Knitted Wraps & Cover-Ups

Annie Modesitt

STACKPOLE BOOKS

0 11557 01444 0

Published by
STACKPOLE BOOKS
5067 Ritter Road
Mechanicsburg, PA 17055
www.stackpolebooks.com

Printed in United States of America

10 9 8 7 6 5 4 3 2 1

First edition

Cover design by Caroline Stover

Photography by Lara Neel, except photos on pages 68 and 70
by Annie Modesitt

Library of Congress Cataloging-in-Publication Data

Modesitt, Annie.
  Knitted wraps & cover-ups : 24 stylish designs for boleros,
capes,
shrugs, crop tops, & more / Annie Modesitt. — First edition.
    pages cm
 Includes index.
  ISBN 978-0-8117-1444-0
1. Knitting—Patterns. 2. Knitwear. I. Title. II. Title: Knitted
wraps and cover-ups.
  TT825.M615 2016
  746.43'2—dc23
                        2015004662

Contents

Introduction

We love small things. We love cute, compact pieces cunningly crafted to cover the chilly contours of a shoulder, neck, or arm.

As knitters, we have a bit of a quandary. We love knitting useful garments to keep us (and our loved ones) warm and comfortable, but often we don't like to commit to a very large project. Socks are fun, scarves and hats are wonderful, but sometimes a tiny bit of a sweater is just what the knitting doctor ordered.

The humble size of a bolero can trick the mind into believing it is utterly ingenuous. But sometimes small things are uniquely sophisticated in their simplicity.

With a few exceptions, the patterns in this book are moderate to smaller sized pieces designed to warm a chilly neck at the office, snug around bare shoulders in a restaurant, or offer a bit of coziness when out for an evening stroll.

I think of these designs as "partial sweaters." Boleros, armerys, shrugs, and shawls are all names for pieces that are fun, relatively quick to knit up, and serve a specific function.

I've attempted to design items which are useful, can be easily sized larger or smaller, and—most of all—are fun to knit! I'd wear any of them (and often do) and I hope my readers find them as enjoyable to knit and wear as I do.

WELCOME TO ALL KNITTERS

As a designer and pattern writer, I strive to create patterns that are democratically written—patterns that anyone can use, which don't exclude any style of knitting (there are more styles than you may know: Eastern, Combination, Left-Handed, and Portuguese, to name a few). To this end, certain knitting terms used in this book may be new to some knitters. As a rule, I try to use knitting terms that describe the *final result* of a technique, not *how to work* the technique, since the "how" varies across different styles of knitting but the results desired are the same. The terms I use that may be new to you are not difficult to understand and should equate easily to what you already know. For more information on different knitting styles and terminology, see How To Use This Book on page 117.

Basketweave Bolero

To create the basketweave pattern, square areas of stockinette stitch are juxtaposed with reverse stockinette stitch, divided by a few rows of garter stitch. This creates a drapey, simple fabric which flows around the body in an easy, flattering way.

Sizes

To fit bust 28 (36, 44, 58)"/71 (92, 112, 148) cm

Finished Measurements

Width: 24 (28, 32, 36)"/61 (71, 82, 92) cm
Length: 35 (43, 51, 59)"/89 (110, 130, 151) cm

Skill Level

Easy

Yarn

Eden Cottage Langdale Superwash Aran, medium weight #4 yarn (100% merino; 180 yd./166 m per 3.5 oz./100 g skein)
• 5 (7, 9, 13) skeins Copper Beech

Needles and Other Materials

• US 8 (5 mm) needles

Gauge

16 sts x 24 rows in St st = 4"/10 cm square
Adjust needle size if necessary to obtain gauge.

Stitch Guide

Dkss Edge (double knit slipped st edge, worked over 3 sts)
This edging is created by slipping and knitting stitches, keeping in mind that whenever stitches are slipped at either 3-st edge, the yarn is held *toward* the knitter, regardless of whether the right or wrong side is facing the knitter. On the RS rows, at either end, the 3 edge sts are worked knit, slip, knit. On the WS rows, at either end, the 3 edge sts are worked slip, knit, slip.
RS Row: {K1, wyrs sl 1, k1}, work to last 3 sts, {k1, wyrs sl 1, k1}.
WS Row: {Wyws sl 1, k1, wyws sl 1}, work to last 3 sts, {wyws sl 1, k1, wyws sl 1}.

Wyrs sl 1 (with yarn right side, slip 1)
Move yarn to RS of work. Insert RH needle purlwise into st and slip off of LH needle.

Wyws sl 1 (with yarn wrong side, slip 1)
Move yarn to WS of work. Insert RH needle purlwise into st and slip off of LH needle.

Jacket

CO 106 (122, 138, 154) sts.
Knit 4 rows.

BEGIN BASKETWEAVE PATTERN

Follow Chart or written instructions as foll:
Row 1 (RS): {K1, wyrs sl 1, k1}, p2, [k16] rep 6 (7, 8, 9) times to last 5 sts, p2, {k1, wyrs sl 1, k1}.

St st   Sl st (wyws)
Rev St St   Sl st (wyrs)

Basketweave Chart

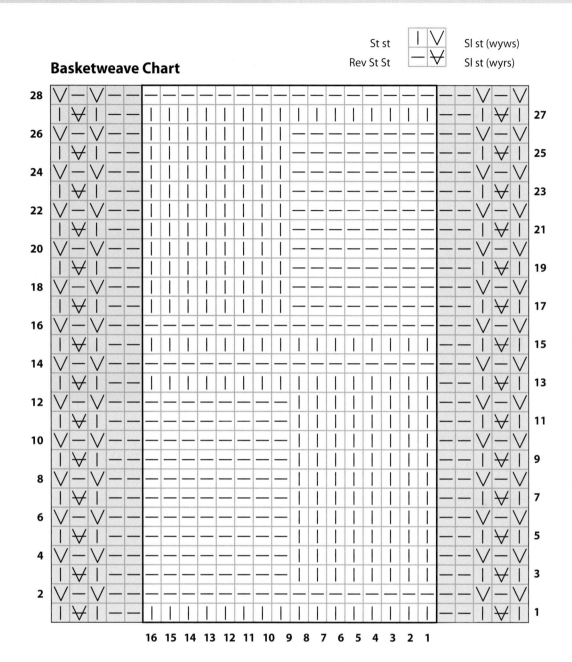

Row 2 (WS): {Wyws sl 1, k1, wyws sl 1}, k2, [k16] rep to last 5 sts, k2, {wyws sl 1, k1, wyws sl 1}.

Row 3: {Dkss edge}, k1, wyrs sl 1, k1, p2, [k8, p8] rep 6 (7, 8, 9) times to last 5 sts, p2, {dkss edge}.

Row 4: {Dkss edge}, k2, [p8, k8] rep 6 (7, 8, 9) times to last 5 sts, k2, {dkss edge}.

Rows 5–12: Rep last 2 rows 8 times more (10 rows total).

Rows 13–16: Rep Rows 1–2 twice.

Row 17: {Dkss edge}, p2, [p8, k8] rep 6 (7, 8, 9) times to last 5 sts, p2, {dkss edge}.

Row 18: {Dkss edge}, k2, [k8, p8] rep 6 (7, 8, 9) times to last 5 sts, k2, {dkss edge}.

Rows 19–26: Rep last 2 rows 8 times more (10 rows total).

Rows 27–28: Rep Rows 1–2.

Rep Rows 1–28 until a total of 6 (7, 8, 11) 14-row squares have been worked (ending either at Row 14 or 28).

ARMHOLE PLACEMENT

Cont in patt as est, create the armhole placement by working 37 (45, 53, 53) sts in patt as est. With a piece of waste yarn, k32 (32, 32, 48) sts. Break waste yarn and set aside. Slip these waste yarn sts back onto the left-hand needle, and cont with body yarn, work in basketweave patt as est across the waste yarn sts and to the end of the row.

Cont in patt as est, complete 42 (56, 70, 84) rows (these rows will be the Back of the garment), then work another armhole placement row as previously worked.

Cont in basketweave patt as est until a total of 6 (7, 8, 11) 14-row squares have been worked from the second waste yarn armhole placement (ending either at row 14 or 28). Bind off all sts loosely.

Sleeve (Make 2)

Return to one waste yarn armhole placement and carefully remove the waste yarn while slipping the 32 (32, 32, 48) sts from one edge of the armhole and 31 (31, 31, 47) from the other edge of the armhole onto a circular needle—63 (63, 63, 95) sts total. Join yarn to work and place marker to note start of round. Work in St st (knit every round) until sleeve meas 10 (10½, 11, 11½)"/26 (27, 28, 29) cm, or desired length. Bind off all sts using an I-cord bind-off as follows:

To start, cast on 3 sts at start of row/round.

1. K2, k2tog-L.
2. Slip 3 sts from RH needle back onto LH needle.
3. Pull yarn taut across back of work.
4. Repeat steps 1–3 across work until 3 sts rem.
5. End k3tog-L, tie off last stitch.

Finishing

Use yarn tails from sleeves to tidy up armhole and cuff edges as you weave in the ends. Steam block piece.

Finished Measurements

7 (9.25, 11.75, 11.75)"/
18 (24, 30, 30) cm

14 (16.25, 19.75, 23.25)"/
36 (41, 50, 59) cm

9.25 (11.25, 13.25, 13.25)"/
24 (29, 34, 34) cm

24 (28, 32, 36)"/61 (71, 82, 92) cm

8 (8, 8, 12)"/
20 (20, 20, 31) cm

35 (43, 51, 59)"/89 (110, 130, 151) cm

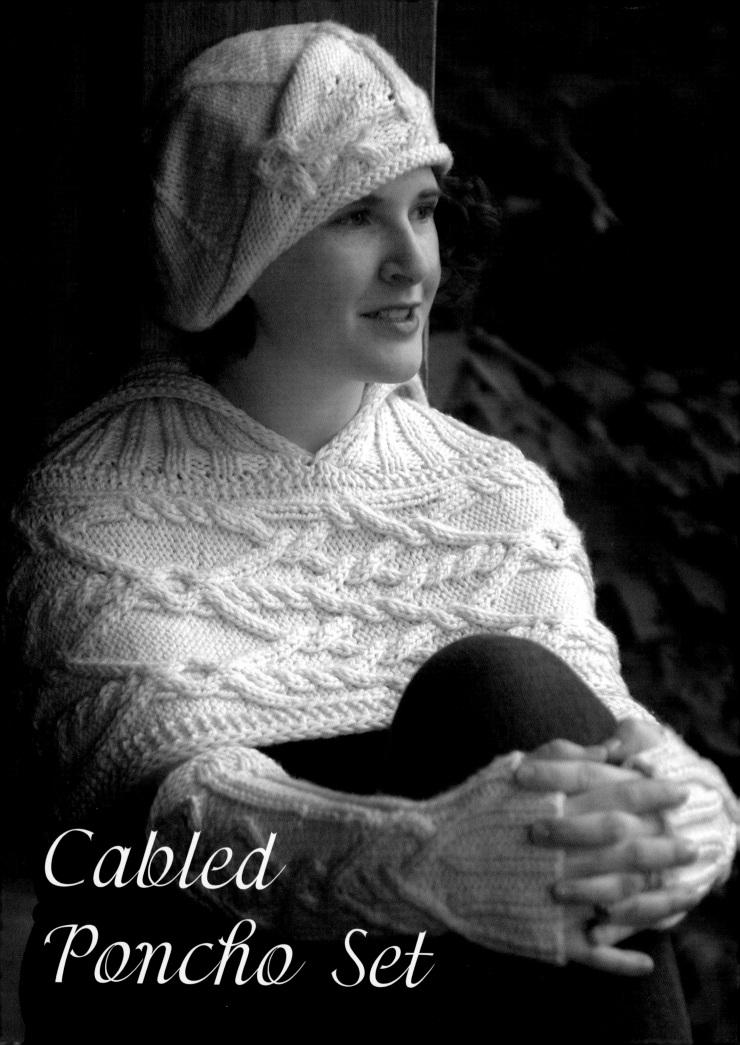

Cabled
Poncho Set

There are few more satisfying moments in knitting than turning a big, beautiful, chunky cable! The only problem with cables is that they can be a bit overwhelming all over a garment.

In this poncho, hat, and gauntlet set, cables are used as a warm and dimensional design element. Because the end product isn't a bulky sweater, fit isn't as much of an issue as it might be, allowing the knitter to settle in and simply enjoy the ride!

There's nothing wrong with using cable needles—many excellent knitters keep them in their toolbox in various lengths and sizes. However, I prefer to knit *all* of my cables without a cable needle (even huge 20-stitch cables!). If you would like to give it a try, I show you how on page 121 and you can watch my video tutorial at http://tinyurl.com/modecable.

Sizes

Poncho: One Size
Gauntlets: Women's Small, Medium, and Large
Hat: Small, Medium, and Large

Finished Measurements

Poncho bust: $44^3/_4$"/114 cm
Poncho length: $13^3/_4$"/35 cm
Gauntlet wrist circumference: 8 ($9^1/_2$, 11)"/20 (24, 28) cm
Gauntlet arm circumference: $9^1/_2$ (11, $12^1/_4$)"/24 (28, 31) cm
Hat head circumference: 17 ($21^1/_4$, $25^1/_2$)"/43 (54, 65) cm

Skill Level

Advanced

Yarn

ModeKnit Yarn ModeWerk Bulky, bulky weight #5 yarn (100% superwash merino; 106 yd./97 m per 3.5 oz./100 g skein)
- Poncho: 4 balls Pearl
- Gauntlets: 2 balls Pearl
- Hat: 2 balls Pearl

Needles and Other Materials

- US 9 (5.5 mm) needles
- US 7 (4.5 mm) needles
- Stitch markers

Gauge

14 sts x 20 rows in Cable patt with US 9 (5.5 mm) needles = 4"/10 cm
Adjust needle size if necessary to obtain gauge.

Stitch Guide

C3pL (cable 3 sts with left twist, purling the back st)
Slip 2 sts and hold to front of work, p1, k slipped st.

C3pR (cable 3 sts with right twist, purling the back st)
Slip 1 st and hold to back of work, k2, purl slipped st.

C4L (cable 4 with a left twist)
Sl 2 sts and hold to front, k2, k slipped sts.

C4R (cable 4 with a right twist)
Move yarn to RS, sl 2 sts and hold to back, k2, k slipped sts.

Dkss Edge (double knit slipped st edge, worked over 3 sts)
This edging is created by slipping and knitting stitches, keeping in mind that whenever stitches are slipped at either 3-st edge, the yarn is held *toward* the knitter, regardless of whether the right or wrong side is facing the knitter. On the RS rows, at either end, the 3 edge sts are worked knit, slip, knit. On the WS rows, at either end, the 3 edge sts are worked slip, knit, slip.

PU (pick up)
Using the knitting needle only, with no source of yarn, pick up a loop from the existing fabric to create a stitch on the needle.

VDD (vertical double decrease)
Sl 2 sts as if to work k2tog-R, k1, pass slipped sts over (decrease of 2 sts).

Wyrs sl 1 (with yarn right side, slip 1)
Move yarn to RS of work. Insert RH needle purlwise into st and slip off of LH needle.

Wyws sl 1 (with yarn wrong side, slip 1)
Move yarn to WS of work. Insert RH needle purlwise into st and slip off of LH needle.

Poncho

One Size
Using any provisional cast-on and with larger needles, CO 48. Work Cabled Poncho Pattern, following chart or written instructions below, repeating Rows 1–56 four times (a total of 224 rows).

CABLED PONCHO PATTERN

Row 1 (RS): K2, p2, [k4, p4] four times, k4, p2, k3. End with dkss RS edge: {K1, wyrs sl 1, k1}.

Rows 2 and 4 (WS): Begin with dkss WS edge: {Wyws sl 1, k1, wyws sl 1}. K5, [p4, k4] five times.

Row 3 (RS): K2, p2, [C4R, p4, C4L, p4] twice, C4R, p2, k3, {dkss RS edge}.

Row 5: K2, p2, k2, [C3pL, p2, C3pR] four times, C3pL, p1, k3, {dkss RS edge}.

continued

Cabled Poncho Chart

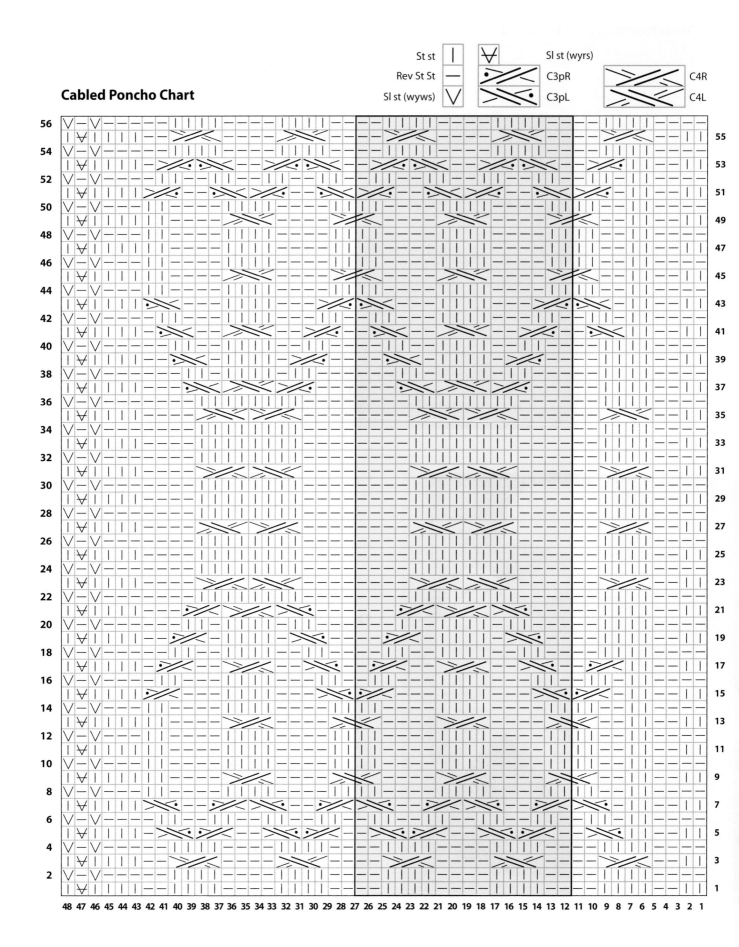

Row 6: {Dkss WS edge}, k4, [p2, k2] eight times, p2, k1, p2, k4.

Row 7: K2, p2, k2, [p1, C3pL, C3pR, p1] four times, p1, C3pL, k3, {dkss RS edge}.

Rows 8, 10, 12, and 14: {Dkss WS edge}, k3, [p2, k4, p2] four times, p2, k2, p2, k4.

Rows 9 and 13: [K2, p2] twice, [C4L, p4, C4R, p4] twice, k5, {dkss RS edge}.

Row 11: [K2, p2] twice, [k4, p4] four times, k5, {dkss RS edge}.

Row 15: K2, p2, k2, [p1, C3pR, C3pL, p3, k4, p2] twice, p1, C3pR, k3, {dkss RS edge}.

Row 16: {Dkss WS edge}, k4, [p2, k3, p4, k3, p2, k2] twice, p2, k1, p2, k4.

Row 17: K2, p2, k2, [C3pR, p2, C3pL, p2, C4R, p2] twice, C3pR, p1, k3, {dkss RS edge}.

Row 18: {Dkss WS edge}, k5, [p2, k2, p4, k2, p2, k4] twice, p4, k4.

Row 19: K2, p2, k4, p2, [p2, C3pL, p1, k4, p1, C3pR, p2] twice, k3, {dkss RS edge}.

Row 20: {Dkss WS edge}, k6, p2, k1, p4, k1, p2, k6, p2, k1, p4, k1, p2, k5, p4, k4.

Row 21: K2, p2, k4, p2, [p3, C3pL, C4R, C3pR, p3] twice, k3, {dkss RS edge}.

Row 22 (and all WS rows to 36): {Dkss WS edge}, k7, p8, k8, p8, k6, p4, k4.

Rows 23 and 31: K2, p2, C4R, p2, [p4, C4L, C4R, p4] twice, k3, {dkss RS edge}.

Rows 25, 29, and 33: K2, p2, k4, p2, [p4, k8, p4] twice, k3, {dkss RS edge}.

Rows 27 and 35: K2, p2, C4L, p2, [p4, C4R, C4L, p4] twice, k3, {dkss RS edge}.

Row 37: K2, p2, k4, p2, [p3, C3pR, C4L, C3pL, p3] twice, k3, {dkss RS edge}.

Row 38: Rep Row 20.

Row 39: K2, p2, k4, p2, [p2, C3pR, p1, k4, p1, C3pL, p2] twice, k3, {dkss RS edge}.

Row 40: {Dkss WS edge}, k5, [p2, k2, p4, k2, p2, k4] twice, p4, k4.

Row 41: K2, p2, k2, [C3pL, p2, C3pR, p2, C4L, p2] twice, C3pL, p1, k3, {dkss RS edge}.

Row 42: {Dkss WS edge}, k4, [p2, k3, p4, k3, p2, k2] twice, p2, k1, p2, k4.

Row 43: K2, p2, k2, [p1, C3pL, C3pR, p3, k4, p2] twice, p1, C3pL, k3, {dkss RS edge}.

Rows 44, 46, 48, and 50: {Dkss WS edge}, k3, [p2, k4, p2] four times, p2, k2, p2, k4.

Rows 45 and 49: [K2, p2] twice, [C4R, p4, C4L, p4] twice, k5, {dkss RS edge}.

Row 47: [K2, p2] twice, [k4, p4] four times, k5, {dkss RS edge}.

Row 51: K2, p2, k2, [p1, C3pR, C3pL, p1] four times, p1, C3pR, k3, {dkss RS edge}.

Row 52: {Dkss WS edge}, k4, [p2, k2] eight times, p2, k1, p2, k4.

Row 53: K2, p2, k2, [C3pR, p2, C3pL] four times, C3pR, p1, k3, {dkss RS edge}.

Rows 54 and 56: {Dkss WS edge}, k5, [p4, k4] five times.

Row 55 (RS): K2, p2, [C4R, p4, C4L, p4] twice, C4R, p2, k3, {dkss RS edge}.

Joining Edges

Carefully slip provisional sts onto circ needle of any size, and, with the Right Sides of the work facing each other, join the CO and last row worked in a 3-needle BO (see page 119 for instructions).

The garter edge of the tube you've just created is the top edge, the dkss edge is the bottom hem. Decide which point should be the center front of the poncho, and begin picking up yoke sts at this place.

YOKE

With smaller needle, PU 112 sts around top edge of tube, 1 st for each garter ridge.

Cont across front, PU 8 more sts in same garter ridges as original 8 sts. This will create an overlap at the center front of the poncho—120 sts.

Working back and forth from this point on, turn work.

Next row (WS): {Wyws sl 1, k1, wyws sl 1}, [k2, p2] rep to last 3 sts, {wyws sl 1, k1, wyws sl 1}.

Next row (RS): {K1, wyrs sl 1, k1}, [K1, wyrs sl 1, k1] work in rib as est to last 3 sts, {k1, wyrs sl 1, k1}.

Cont as est, working either end in dkss edge and working all other sts in rib as est for 12 rows.

Row 1 (RS): {Dkss RS edge}, work 14 as est, k2tog-R, [work 26 in rib as est, k2tog-R] three times, work rem 14 as est, {dkss RS edge}—116 sts.

Row 2 and all WS rows: Work in dkss edge and rib as est.

Row 3 (RS): [Work as est to dec st from prev RS row, sl 1] four times, work to end of row as est.

Row 4: Work in dkss edge and rib as est.

Row 5 (RS): [Work as est to 1 st before slipped st from prev RS row, VDD] four times, work as est to end of row—108 sts.

Row 6: Work in dkss edge and rib as est.

Rep Rows 3–6, decreasing 8 sts every 4th round, until 68 sts rem.

Work even in rib as est, cont to slip the st in the decrease course every RS row until yoke meas 10"/25.5 cm from pick up point.

BO all sts using an I-cord bind-off as follows.

To start, cast on 3 sts at start of row/round.

1. K2, k2tog-L.
2. Slip 3 sts from RH needle back onto LH needle.
3. Pull yarn taut across back of work.
4. Repeat steps 1–3 across work until 3 sts rem.
5. End k3tog-L, tie off last stitch.

Weave in ends.

Finished Measurements

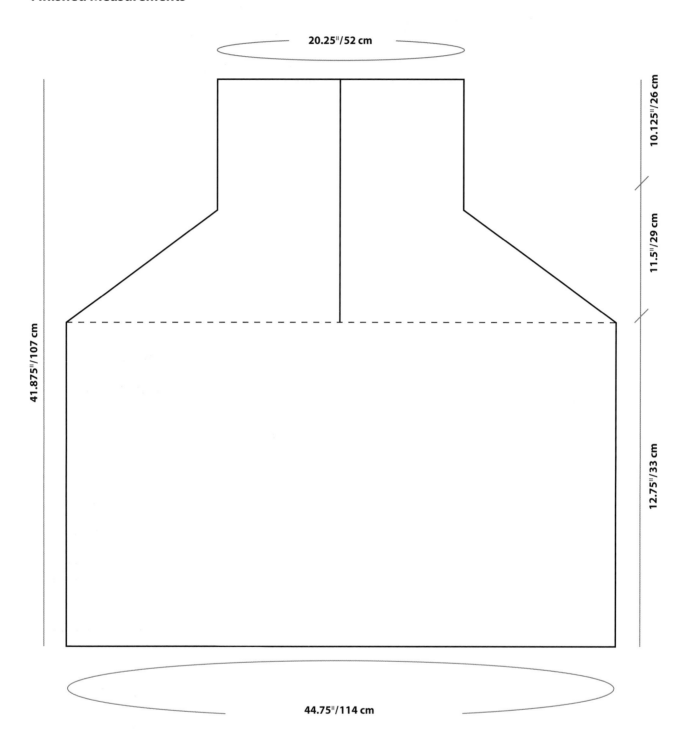

20.25"/52 cm

10.125"/26 cm

11.5"/29 cm

41.875"/107 cm

12.75"/33 cm

44.75"/114 cm

Cabled Gauntlet and Hat Chart

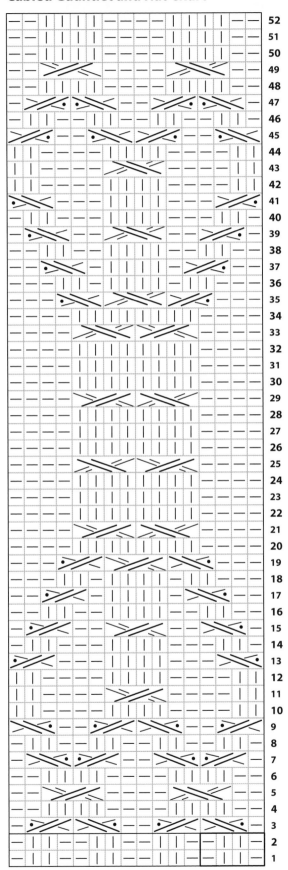

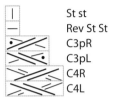

	St st
—	Rev St St
⤬	C3pR
⤬	C3pL
⤬	C4R
⤬	C4L

Gauntlet

Sizes: Small (Medium, Large)

With smaller needles CO 32 (36, 40) sts. Join to work in the round, and est ribbing as foll:

Rnd 1 *(Sizes S and L)*: K1, [p2, k2] rep to last st, end k1. Place marker to note start of round.

Rnd 1 *(Size M)*: P1, [k2, p2] rep to last st, end p1. Place marker to note start of round.

Rnd 2: Work in rib as est.

Cont in rib as est for 6 rounds total.

Thumb Placement

Left

Next rnd: Work 5 (7, 9) sts in rib as est, BO next 3 sts, cont in rib as est.

Next rnd: Work to BO sts, CO 3 sts, work to end of round in rib.

Cont in rib as est, working rib in newly CO sts. Work until piece meas 3"/7.5 cm from CO, or desired length to wrist.

Right

Work the BO sts 24 (26, 28) from start of round. Work CO as for Left Gauntlet.

HAND

Work 8 (10, 12) sts in rib, ending with a purl st. Place marker. Work Row 1 of Cabled Gauntlet and Hat Pattern, using written instructions or chart, across next 16 sts, place marker, work rem 8 (10, 12) sts in rib as est.

Cont in rib as est on either side of center sts, while working all 50 rows of Cabled Gauntlet and Hat Pattern in center 16 sts only *at the same time* inc 1 st on either side of center 16 sts every 8th row as foll:

Inc Round: K to 1 st before marker, kfb, slip marker, work in patt as est to next marker, slip marker, kfb, work in rib as est to end of round.

continued

Inc in this manner every 8th round until there are a total of 36 (40, 44) sts.

Work even with no further increasing to Row 50 of chart. Repeat, beg with Row 3 of chart and work to desired length (to elbow).

BO all sts using an I-cord bind-off as described for the poncho on page 9.

CABLED GAUNTLET AND HAT CHART WRITTEN INSTRUCTIONS

Note: Use this 16-st pattern/chart once across for the center panel of the Gauntlet. For the Hat, you will repeat the 16 sts between each set of markers around.

Rnds 1–2: P1 [k2, p1] four times.
Rnd 3: [P1, C3pL, C3pR, p1] rep around.
Rnd 4: [P2, k4, p2] two times.
Rnd 5: [P2, C4L, p2] two times.
Rnd 6: Rep Rnd 4.
Rnd 7: [P1, C3pR, C3pL, p1] two times.
Rnd 8: [P1, k2, p1] four times.
Rnd 9: [C3pR, p2, C3pL] two times.
Rnd 10: [K2, p4, k2] two times.
Rnd 11: K2, p4, C4R, p4, k2.
Rnd 12: [K2, p4, k2] two times.
Rnd 13: C3pL, p3, k4, p3, C3pR.
Rnd 14: P1, k2, p3, k4, p3, k2, p1.
Rnd 15: P1, C3pL, p2, C4R, p2, C3pR, p1.
Rnd 16: P2, k2, p2, k4, p2, k2, p2.
Rnd 17: P2, C3pL, p1, k4, p1, C3pR, p2.
Rnd 18: P3, k2, p1, k4, p1, k2, p3.
Rnd 19: P3, C3pL, C4R, C3pR, p3.
Rnd 20: P4, k8, p4.
Rnd 21: P4, C4L, C4R, p4.
Rnds 22–24: P4, k8, p4.
Rnd 25: P4, C4R, C4L, p4.
Rnds 26–28: P4, k8, p4.
Rnd 29: P4, C4L, C4R, p4.
Rnds 30–32: P4, k8, p4.
Rnd 33: P4, C4R, C4L, p4.
Rnd 34: P4, k8, p4.
Rnd 35: P3, C3pR, C4L, C3pL, p3.
Rnd 36: P3, k2, p1, k4, p1, k2, p3.
Rnd 37: P2, C3pR, p1, k4, p1, C3pL, p2.
Rnd 38: P2, k2, p2, k4, p2, k2, p2.
Rnd 39: P1, C3pR, p2, C4L, p2, C3pL, p1.
Rnd 40: P1, k2, p3, k4, p3, k2, p1.
Rnd 41: C3pR, p3, k4, p3, C3pL.
Rnd 42: [K2, p4, k2] two times.
Rnd 43: K2, p4, C4L, p4, k2.
Rnd 44: K2, p4, k2 two times.
Rnd 45: C3pL, p2, C3pR, C3pL, p2, C3pR.
Rnd 46: [P1, k2, p1] four times.
Rnd 47: P1, C3pL, C3pR, p2, C3pL, C3pR, p1.
Rnd 48: [P2, k4, p2] two times.
Rnd 49: P2, C4L, p4, C4R, p2.
Rnds 50–51: [P2, k4, p2] two times.

Hat

Sizes: Small (Medium, Large)

With smaller needles, CO 64 (80, 96) sts. Join to work in the round.

Knit 6 rounds (St st) to create a rolled brim.

Begin Charted Pattern

Rnd 1: Change to larger needles and work Rnd 1 of Gauntlet Chart around all sts 4 (5, 6) times, placing a marker between each repeat. Place contrasting marker to note start of round—4 (5, 6) markers.

Cont working in charted patt as est to round 8 of chart.

Rnd 9: [Slip marker, yo, work in charted patt as est to next marker] rep around—68 (85, 102) sts.

Rnds 10–12: Work in charted patt as est, purling the extra stitch created by the yo in Rnd 9.

Rnd 13: [Slip marker, P1, yo, cont in patt as est to st before next marker, p1, yo (2 yo's in each section)—76 (95, 114) sts.

Rnds 14–16: Work in charted patt as est, purling the extra sts created by the yos in Rnd 13.

Rnd 17: Work as for Rnd 13—84 (105, 126) sts.

Rnds 18–20: Work in charted patt as est, purling the extra sts created by the yos in Rnd 17.

Rnd 21: Work as for Rnd 13—92 (115, 138) sts, 23 sts in each section.

Cont working in charted patt as est, incorporating the new sts into the purl section between the cable patt in each section. Work to Round 22 (26, 30), or to desired depth.

> **TIP:** Work to 1 st before next marker, carefully lift next st off left-hand needle and remove marker, then replace stitch.

Decreases

Rnd 1: Work a VDD over next 3 sts (center stitch of decrease corresponds to the first stitch of the section). Knit around the work, removing all markers and working a VDD at each former marker point—21 sts rem in each section, 84 (105, 126) sts total.

Rnds 2–3: Knit all sts.

Rnd 4: [Knit to 1 st before the next VDD from 2 rows below, VDD] rep around work—19 sts rem in each section, 76 (95, 114) sts total.

Rep the last 3 rounds, working a VDD every 3rd round until 4 (5, 6) sts rem. Break yarn, draw through rem sts, tie off.

Chevron Cowled Poncho

The chevron pattern in this garment highlights the beautifully dyed variegated yarn, adding a bit of interest and texture within an easy-to-memorize stitch pattern. The garment decreases within the pattern, then at the neck a whole *new* sock-weight yarn is added to create a frothy, light, cowl-type collar.

Sizes

To fit chest 30 (36, 42, 48)"/77 (92, 107, 122) cm

Finished Measurements

Hem circumference: 60 (66, 72, 78)"/153 (168, 184, 199) cm
Total length: 18 (18³/₄, 19¹/₄, 20)"/46 (48, 49, 51) cm

Skill Level

Intermediate

Yarn

ModeKnit Yarn ModeWerk Bulky, bulky weight #5 yarn (100% superwash merino; 106 yd./97 m per 3.5 oz./100 g ball)
• 3 (4, 5, 6) balls Gilmarite (Yarn A)
ModeKnit Yarn ModeSock, super fine #1 weight yarn (60% superwash merino, 30% bamboo, 10% nylon; 382yd./348 m per 3.5oz./100 g ball)
• 1 (1, 1, 1) ball Gilmarite (Yarn B)

Needles and Other Materials

• US 9 (5.5 mm) needles
• US 6 (4 mm) needles
• Stitch markers

Gauge

16 sts x 24 rows in Chevron Patt on US 9 needles = 4"/10 cm square
Adjust needle sizes if necessary to obtain gauge.

Stitch Guide

K2tog-L (knit 2 tog with a left slant)

Knit 2 stitches together so the working needle is pointing to the left as it enters the stitch (dec will slant to the left); common left-slanting decreases are ssk, k2tog-tbl, or skp.

VDD (vertical double decrease)

Sl 2 sts as if to work k2tog-R, k1, pass slipped sts over (decrease of 2 sts).

VQD (vertical quad decrease)

Sl 3 sts as if to work k3tog-R, k2tog-L, pass slipped sts over knit st (decrease of 4 sts).

Body

With larger needles and Yarn A, CO 240 (264, 288, 312) sts.
Rnd 1: [(P2, k2) six times, place marker] 10 (11, 12, 13) times around work, placing contrasting marker to note end of round.
Rnds 2–14: Work in ribbing as est.
Rnd 15: [K11, k2tog-L, k10, yo, k1] 10 (11, 12, 13) times around work.
Rnd 16: Knit all sts.

BEGIN CHEVRON PATT

Rnd 17: [Yo, k10, VDD, k10, yo, k1] 10 (11, 12, 13) times around work.
Rnd 18: Knit all sts.
Rep last 2 rnds 32 (34, 36, 38) times more—64 (68, 72, 76) rnds total.

SHOULDER DECREASES

Following Rnd 19 of Chevron Poncho Chart, work dec as foll:
Rnd 19: [Yo, k to 2 sts before dec from two rnds previous, VQD, k to 2 sts before marker, yo, k1] 10 (11, 12, 13) times around work—220 (242, 264, 286) sts.
Rnds 20 and 22: Knit.
Rnd 23: Yo, k to 1 st before dec from two rnds previous, VDD, k to 2 sts before marker, yo, k1] 10 (11, 12, 13) times around work.
Rep the last 4 rounds until 80 (88, 96, 104) sts rem on needles, 8 each in 10 (11, 12, 13) sections.
Rnd 51: [K2, p2] rep around work, removing all markers.

Chevron Poncho

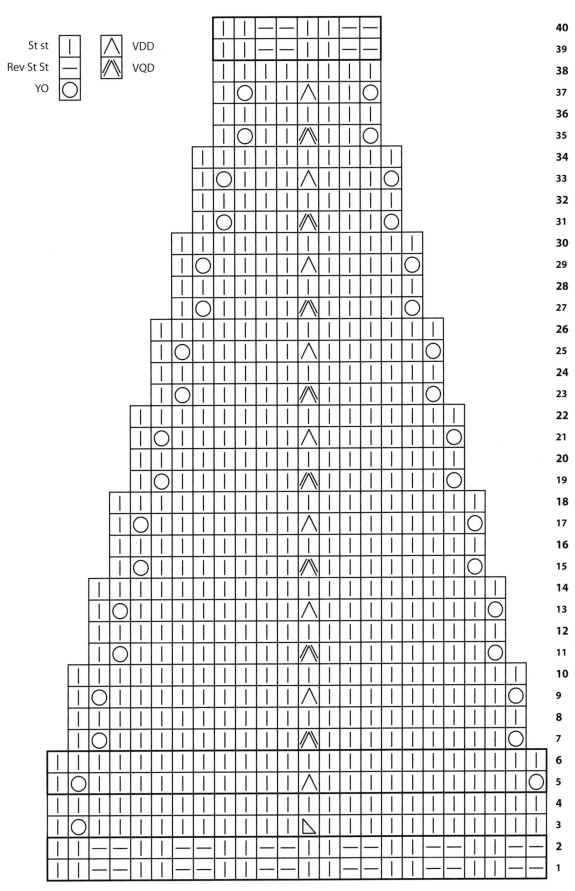

Cowl

With smaller needle and Yarn B, working with the 80 (88, 96, 104) sts on the needle, [k1, kfb] around work—120 (132, 144, 156) sts.

Work in St st, knitting all sts, until cowl meas $5^1/4$ (6, $6^3/4$, $7^1/4$)"/13 (15, 17, 18) cm from start (or desired length).

Next rnd: Purl.

Next rnd: Knit.

Rep last 2 rnds once more.

Bind off all sts using a picot bind-off as follows (see page 120 for photo-illustrated instructions):
1. K2tog-L.

2. Slip the st created back onto the LH needle and knit it.
3. Slip the st just created back onto the LH needle and knit it.
4. Slip the stitch created back onto the LH needle and work it, together with the next st, as a k2tog-L.

Rep steps 2–4 around work until all sts are bound off.

Finishing

Weave in ends. Steam block piece.

Finished Measurements

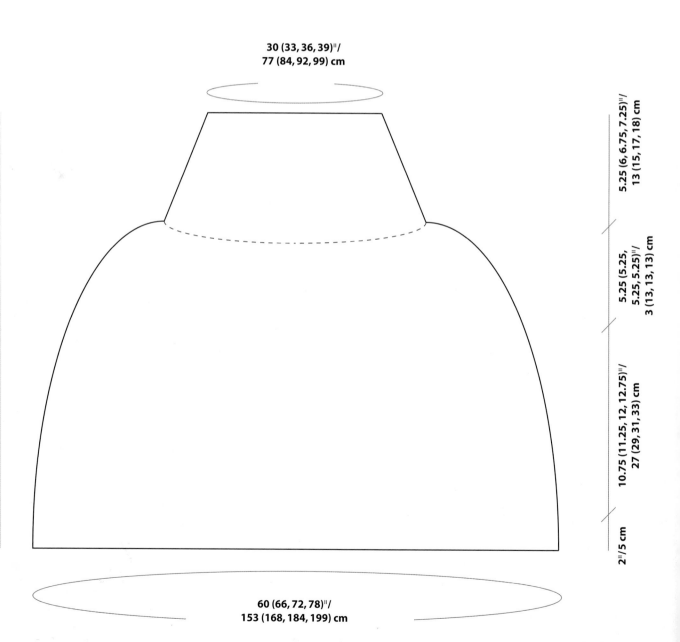

30 (33, 36, 39)"/
77 (84, 92, 99) cm

5.25 (6, 6.75, 7.25)"/
13 (15, 17, 18) cm

5.25 (5.25, 5.25, 5.25)"/
3 (13, 13, 13) cm

18 (18.75, 19.25, 20)"/46 (48, 49, 51) cm

10.75 (11.25, 12, 12.75)"/
27 (29, 31, 33) cm

2"/5 cm

60 (66, 72, 78)"/
153 (168, 184, 199) cm

Colorwork Ruana

The Triple Twist Drop Stitch is an exciting little technique which really shows off the yarn used in the garment. This is definitely something to practice a bit before actually casting on, but once the knitter has "mistressed" the technique, it will become a firm favorite! The shape of the garment is incredibly simple—just three rectangles—so I've chosen a very simple single crochet edge to complement and anchor the garment.

Sizes

To fit bust 28 (38, 48, 58)"/71 (97, 122, 148) cm

Finished Measurements

Back width: 37³/₄ (47, 56¹/₂, 66)"/96 (120, 144, 168) cm
Total length: 20¹/₄ (24¹/₂, 26, 30¹/₄)"/52 (63, 66, 77) cm

Skill Level

Intermediate

Yarn

Sincere Sheep Equity Sport, fine weight #2 yarn (100% wool; 225 yd./233 m per 2 oz./57 g ball)
- 2 (3, 5, 7) balls Kung Hei Fat Choi (Color A)
- 1 (2, 2, 3) balls Mrs. Fisher (Color B)
- 1 (2, 2, 3) balls Prayer to Artemis (Color C)
- 1 (2, 2, 3) balls Virid (Color D)
- 1 (2, 2, 3) balls Leopard Anja (Color E)

Needles and Other Materials

- US 7 (4.5 mm) needles
- US E-4 (3.5 mm) crochet hook

Gauge

17 sts x 26 rows in St st = 4"/10 cm square
Adjust needle size if necessary to obtain gauge.

Stitch Guide

Hdc (half double crochet)

Yarn over hook. Insert hook in the next stitch to be worked. Yarn over hook. Pull yarn through stitch. Yarn over hook. Pull yarn through all 3 loops on hook (one half double crochet made).

Sc (single crochet)

Insert hook in stitch. Yarn over hook. Pull yarn through stitch. Yarn over hook. Pull yarn through 2 loops on hook (one single crochet made).

Sl St (slip stitch)

Move yarn to WS of work. Insert RH needle purlwise into st and slip off LH needle.

Triple Twist Drop Stitch

Insert needle into next st and wrap yarn three times around *both* needles, then yo around RH needle and draw yo through all of the wraps, allowing all wrapped loops to fall off of ends of needle. Do *not* pull the stitch tight or adjust tension until next row.

Triple Twist Drop Stitch

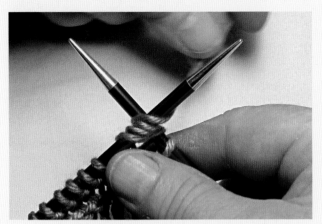

1. Insert RH needle into stitch, form an X, and wrap yarn around both needles three times.

2. Yo around RH needle only.

3. Pull loop through three wraps and stitch.

4. Don't pull the yarn tight or try to adjust tension.

5. Work 2 rows of garter before attempting to straighten the rows. In this photo, the rows have been blocked.

Back

With A, CO 160 (200, 240, 280) sts. Work 3 rows in garter st (knit every row), ending with a RS row, ready to work a WS row (Rows 1–3 of Colorwork Ruana Chart).

BEGIN HEM PATTERN

Cont in chart as est, rep Rows 4–23 as foll:

Row 4 (WS): Drop A. With B [sl 1, k1] rep across work, end sl 1.

Rows 5 and 7 (RS): Purl.

Row 6 (WS): Knit.

Row 8 (WS): With A [k1, p1] rep across work, end k1.

Row 9 (RS): Drop A. With C [sl 1, k1] rep across work, end sl 1.

Rows 10 and 12 (WS): Purl.

Row 11 (RS): Knit.

Row 13 (RS): With A [p1, k1] rep across work, end p1.

Row 14 (WS): With D, rep Row 4.

Rows 15–17: With D, rep Rows 5–7.

Row 18 (WS): Rep Row 8.

Row 19 (RS): With E, rep Row 9.

Rows 20–22: With E, rep Rows 10–12.

Row 23 (RS): Rep Row 13.

Rep [Rows 4–23] 3 (3$\frac{1}{2}$, 4, 4$\frac{1}{2}$) times [60 (70, 80, 90) rows total], or until edge piece meas 9$\frac{1}{4}$ (10$\frac{3}{4}$, 12$\frac{1}{4}$, 13$\frac{3}{4}$)"/24 (27, 31, 35) cm from cast on. End with Row 23 or 13.

DROPPED STITCH SECTION

Cont in chart as est, the next row should be a WS row.

Row 24: Cont with A, knit.

Row 25 (RS): With B, work 160 (200, 240, 280) Triple Twist Drop Sts across work.

Row 26 (WS): Rep Row 25, cut working yarn, leaving an 8"/20 cm tail (do not cut A).

Row 27 (RS): With A, knit.

Row 28 (WS): With A, knit.

Rep Rows 25–27, exchanging colors C, D, and E in place of B in each subsequent repeat.

Work in this manner until Dropped Stitch Section meas 11 (13$\frac{3}{4}$, 13$\frac{3}{4}$, 16$\frac{1}{2}$)"/28 (35, 35, 42) cm, ending with Row 27 (a RS row). Do not bind off sts; slip to holder or waste yarn to work later.

Front (Make 2)

With A, CO 80 (100, 120, 140) sts. Work 3 rows in garter st (knit every row), ending with a RS row, ready to work a WS row. (Rows 1–3 of chart).

Work exactly as for Back, ending at the same point. Slip all Front onto one needle if they're not already.

Colorwork Ruana Chart

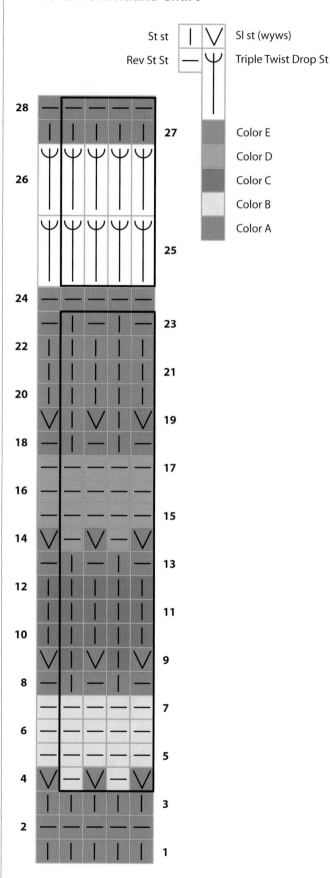

St st	│	V Sl st (wyws)
Rev St St	—	Triple Twist Drop St

Color E
Color D
Color C
Color B
Color A

Joining Fronts and Back

Slip Back sts onto needle and adjust work so that the Front sts are on one needle with the Right Side facing toward the Right Side of the Back. The stitches should be parallel on two needles. Join all sts using a 3-needle bind-off.

EDGING

Row 1 (RS): With a strand of A and beg at the lower left side front corner, work 132 (159, 169, 197) single crochets along the left edge. Work 1 sc into each standard row, work 3 sc into each Triple Drop Stitch row.

Row 2 (WS): Work 1 hdc into each sc.
Row 3 (RS): Work 1 hdc into each hdc.
Row 4 (WS): Work 1 sc into each hdc. Tie off last st.
Repeat Edging for Right Side of work.
Repeat Edging around Neck Edge sts.

Finishing

Weave in ends. Steam block piece.

Finished Measurements

18.75 (23.5, 28.25, 33)″/48 (60, 72, 84) cm

11 (11.75, 13.75, 16.5)″/28 (35, 35, 42) cm

9.25 (10.75, 12.25, 13.75)″/24 (27, 31, 35) cm

20.25 (24.5, 26, 30.25)″/52 (63, 66, 77) cm

37.75 (47, 56.5, 66)″/96 (120, 144, 168) cm

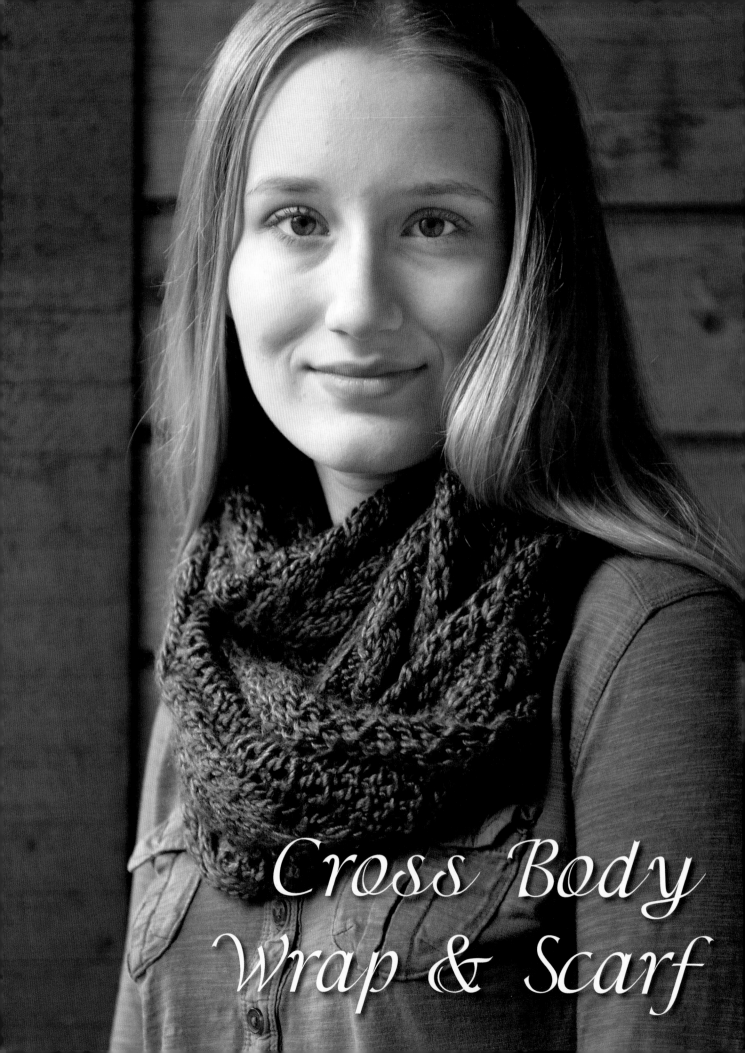

Cross Body
Wrap & Scarf

This wrap is a blast to knit up, and just as much fun to wear! It's worked in one long scarf-like piece, then joined with a single twist to allow it to hug the body like a clingy vest. The piece can also be worn as an infinity scarf or pulled over the head, hood-like, for a bit of extra drama.

Sizes

One Size

Finished Measurements

Width: 12³/₄"/33 cm
Length: 60¹/₂"/154 cm

Skill Level

Intermediate

Yarn

Fyberspates Scrumptious DK Worsted (55% merino, 45% silk; 241 yd./220 m per 3.5 oz./100 g skein)
• 3 skeins Slate Grey

Needles and Other Materials

• US 7 (4.5 mm) needles

Gauge

14 sts x 18 rows in St st = 4"/10 cm square
Adjust needle size if necessary to obtain gauge.

Stitch Guide

C4L (cable 4 with a left twist)
Sl 2 sts and hold to front, k2, k slipped sts.

C4R (cable 4 with a right twist)
Move yarn to RS, sl 2 sts and hold to back, k2, k slipped sts.

C11 Center
Sl 5 sts and hold to back, sl 1 st to second cable needle and hold to front, k5, k1 from front cable needle, k5 from back cable needle.

Dkss Edge (double knit slipped st edge, worked over 3 sts)
This edging is created by slipping and knitting stitches, keeping in mind that whenever stitches are slipped at either 3-st edge, the yarn is held *toward* the knitter, regardless of whether the right or wrong side is facing the knitter. On the RS rows, at either end, the 3 edge sts

are worked knit, slip, knit. On the WS rows, at either end, the 3 edge sts are worked slip, knit, slip.
RS Row: {K1, wyrs sl 1, k1}, work to last 3 sts, {k1, wyrs sl 1, k1}.
WS Row: {Wyws sl 1, k1, wyws sl 1}, work to last 3 sts, {wyws sl 1, k1, wyws sl 1}.

K2tog-L (knit 2 tog with a left slant)
Knit 2 stitches together so the working needle is pointing to the left as it enters the stitch (dec will slant to the left); common left-slanting decreases are ssk, k2tog-tbl, or skp.

K2tog-R (knit 2 tog with a right slant)
Knit 2 stitches together so the working needle is pointing to the right as it enters the stitch (dec will slant to the right); most common is k2tog.

P2tog (purl 2 tog)
Working on WS of piece, insert needle into 2 stitches from back to front, yo, pull loop through both stitches and kick old stitches off of needle. Decreased stitches will slant to the right when viewed from RS of work.

P2tog-tbl (purl 2 tog through the back loop)
Working on the WS of piece, purl 2 sts together so the working needle is pointing to the right as it enters the sts (needle enters the second st on LH needle, then the first st on LH needle). Decreased stitches will slant to the left when viewed from RS.

Body

Using any provisional CO, cast on 45 sts.
Following Cross Body Wrap Chart or written instructions below, work Rows 1–40 once.
[Work Rows 41–44 once, then work Rows 45–48 six times] repeat these 28 rows four times.
Work Rows 49–86 once, increasing in the center of Row 85 as indicated—46 sts.
Rep [Rows 87–88] 32 times, or until ribbing section is desired length.

Cross Body Wrap Chart

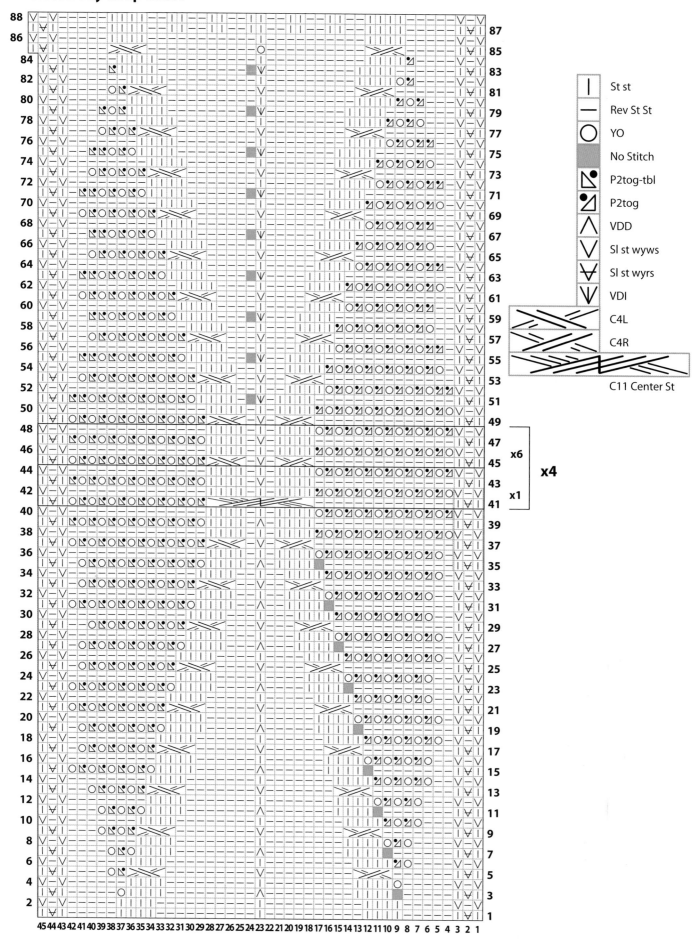

Legend:
- | St st
- — Rev St St
- ○ YO
- ▨ No Stitch
- ◹ P2tog-tbl
- ◸ P2tog
- ∧ VDD
- V Sl st wyws
- ⩝ Sl st wyrs
- W VDI
- C4L
- C4R
- C11 Center St

CROSS BODY WRAP CHART WRITTEN INSTRUCTIONS

Row 1 (RS): {K1, wyrs sl 1, k1}, p5, k4, p10, k1, p10, k4, p5, {k1, wyrs sl 1, k1}.

Row 2 (WS): {Wyws sl 1, k1, wyws sl 1}, k5, p4, k10, p1, k10, p4, k5, {wyws sl 1, k1, wyws sl 1}.

Row 3: {Dkss RS edge}, p5, k4, p9, VDD, p9, k4, yo, p5, {dkss RS edge}.

Row 4: {Dkss WS edge}, k6, p4, k9, p1, k9, p4, yo, k5, {dkss WS edge}.

Row 5: {Dkss RS edge}, p6, C4R, p9, sl 1, p9, C4L, p2tog-tbl, yo, p4, {dkss RS edge}.

Row 6: {Dkss WS edge}, k6, p4, k9, p1, k9, p4, p2tog-R, yo, k4, {dkss WS edge}.

Row 7: {Dkss RS edge}, p6, k4, p8, VDD, p8, k4, yo, p2tog-tbl, yo, p4, {dkss RS edge}.

Row 8: {Dkss WS edge}, k7, p4, k8, p1, k8, p4, yo, p2tog-R, yo, k4, {dkss WS edge}.

Row 9: {Dkss RS edge}, p7, C4R, p8, sl 1, p8, C4L, [p2tog-tbl, yo] twice, p3, {dkss RS edge}.

Row 10: {Dkss WS edge}, k7, p4, k8, p1, k8, p4, [p2tog, yo] twice, k3, {dkss WS edge}.

Row 11: {Dkss RS edge}, p7, k4, p7, VDD, p7, k4, yo, [p2tog-tbl, yo] twice, p3, {dkss RS edge}.

Row 12: {Dkss WS edge}, k8, p4, k7, p1, k7, p4, yo, [p2tog, yo] twice, k3, {dkss WS edge}.

Row 13: {Dkss RS edge}, p8, C4R, p7, sl 1, p7, C4L, [p2tog-tbl, yo] three times, p2, {dkss RS edge}.

Row 14: {Dkss WS edge}, k8, p4, k7, p1, k7, p4, [p2tog, yo] three times, k2, {dkss WS edge}.

Row 15: {Dkss RS edge}, p8, k4, p6, VDD, p6, k4, yo, [p2tog-tbl, yo] four times, {dkss RS edge}.

Row 16: {Dkss WS edge}, k9, p4, k6, p1, k6, p4, yo, [p2tog, yo] three times, k2, {dkss WS edge}.

Row 17: {Dkss RS edge}, p9, C4R, p6, sl 1, p6, C4L, [p2tog-tbl, yo] four times, p1, {dkss RS edge}.

Row 18: {Dkss WS edge}, k9, p4, k6, p1, k6, p4, [p2tog, yo] four times, k1, {dkss WS edge}.

Row 19: {Dkss RS edge}, p9, k4, p5, VDD, p5, k4, yo, [p2tog-tbl, yo] four times, p1, {dkss RS edge}.

Row 20: {Dkss WS edge}, k10, p4, k5, p1, k5, p4, yo, [p2tog, yo] four times, k1, {dkss WS edge}.

Row 21: {Dkss RS edge}, p10, C4R, p5, sl 1, p5, C4L, [p2tog-tbl, yo] five times, {dkss RS edge}.

Row 22: {Dkss WS edge}, k10, p4, k5, p1, k5, [p2tog, yo] four times, k2, {dkss WS edge}.

Row 23: {Dkss RS edge}, p10, k4, p4, VDD, p4, k4, yo, [p2tog-tbl, yo] five times, {dkss RS edge}.

Row 24: {Dkss WS edge}, k11, p4, k4, p1, k4, p4, yo, [p2tog, yo] four times, k2, {dkss WS edge}.

Row 25: {Dkss RS edge}, p11, C4R, p4, sl 1, p4, C4L, [p2tog-tbl, yo] five times, p1, {dkss RS edge}.

Row 26: {Dkss WS edge}, k11, p4, k4, p1, k4, p4, [p2tog, yo] five times, k1, {dkss WS edge}.

Row 27: {Dkss RS edge}, p11, k4, p3, VDD, p3, k4, yo, [p2tog-tbl, yo] five times, p1, {dkss RS edge}.

Row 28: {Dkss WS edge}, k12, p4, k3, p1, k3, p4, yo, [p2tog, yo] five times, k1, {dkss WS edge}.

continued

Row 29: {Dkss RS edge}, p12, C4R, p3, sl 1, p3, C4L, [p2tog-tbl, yo] five times, p2, {dkss RS edge}.

Row 30: {Dkss WS edge}, k12, p4, k3, p1, k3, p4, [p2tog, yo] five times, k2, {dkss WS edge}.

Row 31: {Dkss RS edge}, p12, k4, p2, VDD, p2, k4, yo, [p2tog-tbl, yo] six times, {dkss RS edge}.

Row 32: {Dkss WS edge}, k13, p4, k2, p1, k2, p4, yo, [p2tog, yo] five times, k2, {dkss WS edge}.

Row 33: {Dkss RS edge}, p13, C4R, p2, sl 1, p2, C4L, [p2tog-tbl, yo] six times, p1, {dkss RS edge}.

Row 34: {Dkss WS edge}, k13, p4, k2, p1, k2, p4, [p2tog, yo] six times, k1, {dkss WS edge}.

Row 35: {Dkss RS edge}, p13, k4, p1, VDD, p1, yo, k4, yo, [p2tog-tbl, yo] six times, p1, {dkss RS edge}.

Row 36: {Dkss WS edge}, k14, p4, k1, p1, k1, p4, yo, [p2tog, yo] six times, k1, {dkss WS edge}.

Row 37: {Dkss RS edge}, p14, C4R, p1, sl 1, p1, C4L, [p2tog-tbl, yo] seven times, {dkss RS edge}.

Row 38: {Dkss WS edge}, k14, p4, k1, p1, k1, p4, [p2tog, yo] seven times, {dkss WS edge}.

Row 39: {Dkss RS edge}, p14, k4, p1, VDD, p1, k4, [yo, p2tog-tbl] seven times, {dkss RS edge}.

Row 40: {Dkss WS edge}, k14, p4, k1, p1, k1, p4, [yo, p2tog] seven times, {dkss WS edge}.

Row 41: {Dkss RS edge}, p14, C11 Center, [p2tog-tbl, yo] seven times, {dkss RS edge}.

Row 42: {Dkss WS edge}, k14, p4, k1, p1, k1, p4, [p2tog, yo] seven times, {dkss WS edge}.

Row 43: {Dkss RS edge}, p14, k4, p1, sl 1, p1, k4, [yo, p2tog-tbl] seven times, {dkss RS edge}.

Row 44: {Dkss WS edge}, k14, p4, k1, p1, k1, p4, [yo, p2tog] seven times, {dkss WS edge}.

Row 45: {Dkss RS edge}, p14, C4R, p1, sl 1, p1, C4L, [p2tog-tbl, yo] seven times, {dkss RS edge}.

Row 46: {Dkss WS edge}, k14, p4, k1, p1, k1, p4, [p2tog, yo] seven times, {dkss WS edge}.

Row 47: {Dkss RS edge}, p14, k4, p1, sl 1, p1, k4, [yo, p2tog-tbl] seven times, {dkss RS edge}.

Row 48: {Dkss WS edge}, k14, p4, k1, p1, k1, p4, [yo, p2tog] seven times, {dkss WS edge}.

Row 49: {Dkss RS edge}, p14, C4R, p1, sl 1, p1, C4L, [p2tog-tbl, yo] seven times, {dkss RS edge}.

Row 50: {Dkss WS edge}, k14, p4, k1, p1, k1, p4, [p2tog, yo] seven times, {dkss WS edge}.

Row 51: {Dkss RS edge}, p14, k4, p1, VDI, p1, k4, [yo, p2tog-tbl] six times, p2tog-tbl, {dkss RS edge}.

Row 52: {Dkss WS edge}, k13, p4, k2, p1, k2, p4 [yo, p2tog] six times, p2tog, {dkss WS edge}.

Row 53: {Dkss RS edge}, p13, C4R, p2, sl 1, p2, C4L, [p2tog-tbl, yo] six times, p1 {dkss RS edge}.

Row 54: {Dkss WS edge}, k13, p4, k2, p1, k2, p4, [p2tog, yo] six times, k1, {dkss WS edge}.

Row 55: {Dkss RS edge}, p13, k4, p2, VDI, p2, k4, [yo, p2tog-tbl] five times, p2tog-tbl, p1 {dkss RS edge}.

Row 56: {Dkss WS edge}, k12, p4, k3, p1, k3, p4, [yo, p2tog] five times, p2tog, k1, {dkss WS edge}.

Row 57: {Dkss RS edge}, p12, C4R, p3, sl 1, p3, C4L, [p2tog-tbl, yo] five times, p2, {dkss RS edge}.

Row 58: {Dkss WS edge}, k12, p4, k3, p1, k3, p4, [p2tog, yo] five times, k2, {dkss WS edge}.

Row 59: {Dkss RS edge}, p12, k4, p3, VDI, p3, k4, [yo, p2tog-tbl] four times, p2tog-tbl, p2, {dkss RS edge}.

Row 60: {Dkss WS edge}, k11, p4, k4, p1, k4, p4, [yo, p2tog] four times, p2tog, k2, {dkss WS edge}.

Row 61: {Dkss RS edge}, p11, C4R, p4, sl 1, p4, C4L, [p2tog-tbl, yo] five times, p1, {dkss RS edge}.

Row 62: {Dkss WS edge}, k11, p4, k4, p1, k4, p4, [p2tog, yo] five times, k1, {dkss WS edge}.

Row 63: {Dkss RS edge}, p11, k4, p4, VDI, p4, k4, [yo, p2tog-tbl] four times, p2tog-tbl, p1, {dkss RS edge}.

Row 64: {Dkss WS edge}, k10, p4, k5, p1, k5, p4, [yo, p2tog] four times, p2tog, k1, {dkss WS edge}.

Row 65: {Dkss RS edge}, p10, C4R, p5, sl 1, p5, C4L, [p2tog-tbl, yo] four times, p2, {dkss RS edge}.

Row 66: {Dkss WS edge}, k10, p4, k5, p1, k5, p4, [p2tog, yo] four times, k2, {dkss WS edge}.

Row 67: {Dkss RS edge}, p10, k4, p5, VDI, p5, k4, [yo, p2tog-tbl] three times, p2tog-tbl, p2, {dkss RS edge}.

Row 68: {Dkss WS edge}, k9, p4, k6, p1, k6, p4, [yo, p2tog] three times, p2tog, k2, {dkss WS edge}.

Row 69: {Dkss RS edge}, p9, C4R, p6, sl 1, p6, C4L, [p2tog-tbl, yo] four times, p1, {dkss RS edge}.

Row 70: {Dkss WS edge}, k9, p4, k6, p1, k6, p4, [p2tog, yo] four times, k1, {dkss WS edge}.

Row 71: {Dkss RS edge}, p9, k4, p6, VDI, p6, k4, [yo, p2tog-tbl] three times, p2tog-tbl, p1, {dkss RS edge}.

Row 72: {Dkss WS edge}, k8, p4, k7, p1, k7, p4, [yo, p2tog] three times, p2tog, k1, {dkss WS edge}.

Row 73: {Dkss RS edge}, p8, C4R, p7, sl 1, p7, C4L, [p2tog-tbl, yo] three times, p2, {dkss RS edge}.

Row 74: {Dkss WS edge}, k8, p4, k7, p1, k7, p4, [p2tog, yo] three times, k2, {dkss WS edge}.

Row 75: {Dkss RS edge}, p8, k4, p7, VDI, p7, k4, [yo, p2tog-tbl] twice, p2tog-tbl, p2, {dkss RS edge}.

Row 76: {Dkss WS edge}, k7, p4, k8, p1, k8, p4, [yo, p2tog] twice, p2tog, k2, {dkss WS edge}.

Row 77: {Dkss RS edge}, p7, C4R, p8, sl 1, p8, C4L, [p2tog-tbl, yo] twice, p3, {dkss RS edge}.

Row 78: {Dkss WS edge}, k7, p4, k8, p1, k8, p4, [p2tog, yo] twice, k3, {dkss WS edge}.

Row 79: {Dkss RS edge}, p7, k4, p8, VDI, p8, k4, p2tog-tbl, yo, p2tog-tbl, p3, {dkss RS edge}.

Row 80: {Dkss WS edge}, k6, p4, k9, p1, k9, p4, p2tog, yo, p2tog, k3, {dkss WS edge}.

Row 81: {Dkss RS edge}, p6, C4R, p9, sl 1, p9, C4L, p2tog-tbl, yo, p4, {dkss RS edge}.

Row 82: {Dkss WS edge}, k6, p4, k9, p1, k9, p4, p2tog, yo, k4, {dkss WS edge}.

Row 83: {Dkss RS edge}, p6, k4, p9, VDI, p9, k4, p2tog-tbl, p4, {dkss RS edge}.

Row 84: {Dkss WS edge}, k5, p4, k10, p1, k10, p4, p2tog, k4, {dkss WS edge}.

Row 85: {Dkss RS edge}, p5, C4R, p10, yo, p11, C4L, p5, {dkss RS edge}.

Row 86: {Dkss WS edge}, k5, p4, k11, p1, k10, p4, k5, {dkss WS edge}.

Row 87: {Dkss RS edge}, p5, k4, p2, [k2, p2] five times, k4, p5, {dkss RS edge}.

Row 88: {Dkss WS edge}, k5, p4, k2, [p2, k2] five times, p4, k5, {dkss WS edge}.

Finishing

Slip the provisionally CO sts onto a needle, and lay the garment flat.

Turn one end of the garment over, putting a twist in it, then join the edges together (keeping the twist) with a 3-needle bind-off, as follows (see page 119 for photo-illustrated instructions).

1. Place the two pieces to be joined on knitting needles so the right sides of each piece are facing each other with the needles parallel.
2. Insert a third needle one size larger through the leading edge of the first stitch on each needle (knitwise).
3. Knit these stitches together as one, leaving 1 st on RH needle.
4. Repeat steps 2–3; slip the older stitch on RH needle over newer stitch.

Repeat step 4 until all sts are bound off. Cut yarn, pull through last stitch.

Finished Measurements

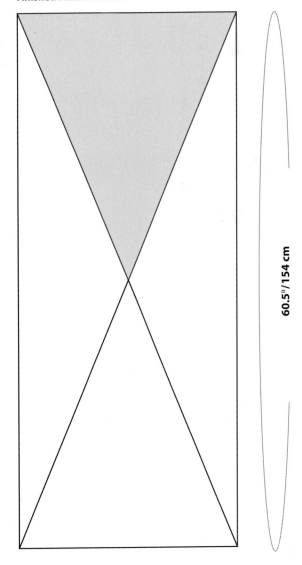

60.5"/154 cm

12.75"/33 cm

Entrelac
Poncho

Entrelac is one of the most fun techniques in knitting! It can be a bit time consuming, but by working through the instructions step by step, you will begin to comprehend the beautiful logic of this piece. Once you wear it a time or two, it is sure to become a memorable mainstay in your wardrobe.

Sizes

To fit bust 30 (36, 42, 48)"/77 (92, 107, 122) cm

Finished Measurements

Neck opening: $16^3/_4$ ($18^1/_2$, $20^3/_4$, $22^1/_2$)"/43 (47, 53, 57) cm
Hem circumference: $46^3/_4$ ($52^1/_2$, 58, $63^1/_2$)"/119 (134, 148, 162) cm

Skill Level

Intermediate

Yarn

Freia Ombre Worsted Wool, medium weight #4 yarn (100% wool; 127 yd./115 m per 2.64 oz./75 g skein)
• 3 skeins Vertigo

Needles and Other Materials

• US 7 (4.5 mm) needles
• US F-5 (3.75 mm) crochet hook to make buttons, or 7 buttons
• Yarn needle

Gauge

20 sts x 32 rows in St st = 4"/10 cm square
Adjust needle size if necessary to obtain gauge.

Stitch Guide

Dkss Edge (double knit slipped st edge, worked over 3 sts)

This edging is created by slipping and knitting stitches, keeping in mind that whenever stitches are slipped at either 3-st edge, the yarn is held *toward* the knitter, regardless of whether the right or wrong side is facing the knitter. On the RS rows, at either end, the 3 edge sts are worked knit, slip, knit. On the WS rows, at either end, the 3 edge sts are worked slip, knit, slip.
RS Row: {K1, wyrs sl 1, k1}, work to last 3 sts, {k1, wyrs sl 1, k1}.
WS Row: {Wyws sl 1, k1, wyws sl 1}, work to last 3 sts, {wyws sl 1, k1, wyws sl 1}.

K2tog-L (knit 2 tog with a left slant)

Knit 2 stitches together so the working needle is pointing to the left as it enters the stitch (dec will slant to the left); common left-slanting decreases are ssk, k2tog-tbl, or skp.

K2tog-R (knit 2 tog with a right slant)

Knit 2 stitches together so the working needle is pointing to the right as it enters the stitch (dec will slant to the right); most common is k2tog.

P2tog (purl 2 tog)

Working on WS of piece, insert needle into 2 stitches from back to front, yo, pull loop through both stitches and kick old stitches off of needle. Decreased stitches will slant to the right when viewed from RS of work.

P2tog-tbl (purl 2 tog through the back loop)

Working on the WS of piece, purl 2 sts together so the working needle is pointing to the right as it enters the sts (needle enters the second st on LH needle, then the first st on LH needle). Decreased stitches will slant to the left when viewed from RS.

PU&K (pick up and knit)

Insert needle into next stitch, stabbing all the way from the right side to the wrong side of the work. Wrap a loop around the needle, pull the loop through, creating a knit stitch.

PU&P (pick up and purl)

Using a separate source of yarn, insert the knitting needle from the back to the front of the work, yo, pull loop through, creating a stitch on the needle.

Kfb (knit into front and back of same stitch)

Knit into the front and back of one stitch, then kick that stitch off the needle—increase of 1 st.

Body

Note: Band One and all odd-numbered bands will be worked as WS bands (working from left to right across the garment). All other bands will be worked as RS bands (working from right to left across the garment). The piece is worked from the neck to the hem, with a 5-st garter edge worked at either side only in the even-numbered bands. Buttonholes are worked on the Left Garter Edge.

NECK EDGE

Using any provisional CO method, CO 106 (118, 130, 142). Knit 2 rows ending with a RS row (the next row will be a WS row).

BAND ONE
6-st WS Triangles—Chart 1

Turn work so WS is facing. K5, place marker. Begin making 6-st triangles as foll:

Row 1 (WS): P2, turn.
Row 2 (RS): K2, turn.
Row 3: P3, turn.
Row 4: K3, turn.
Row 5: P4, turn.
Row 6: K4, turn.
Row 7: P5, turn.
Row 8: K5, turn.
Row 9: P6, turn.
Row 10: K6. *Do **not** turn work!*

Place marker and continue along cast on sts.
Repeating Rows 1–10, create a total of 16 (18, 20, 22) 6-st triangles.
At the end of the row, knit the 5 rem sts—106 (118, 130, 142) total.
Note: The 5 sts at the beg and end of the row will become the button bands.

BAND TWO
6-st Right Edge Triangle (make one at start of band)—Chart 2A

Turn work so RS is facing, k5, sm.
Row 1: (RS) K2, turn.
Row 2: (WS) P2, turn.
Row 3: Kfb (increase of one st), k2tog-L, turn.
Row 4: Sl 1, p2, turn.
Row 5: Kfb, k1, k2tog-L, turn.
Row 6: Sl 1, p3, turn.
Row 7: Kfb, k2, k2tog-L, turn.
Row 8: Sl 1, p4, turn.
Row 9: Kfb, k3, k2tog-L, turn.

Entrelac Poncho Charts

Chart 1
(Establishing triangles)

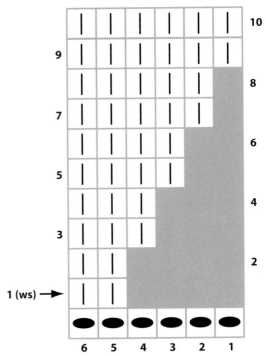

Chart 2A
Beginning Triangle

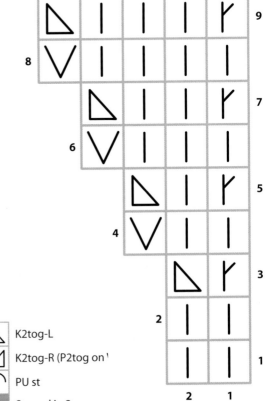

P2tog	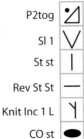
Sl 1	V
St st	│
Rev St St	—
Knit Inc 1 L	Y
CO st	⬬

K2tog-L	◹
K2tog-R (P2tog on '	◸
PU st	⌒
St used in 2 segs	▨

Chart 2B
Center Rectangles

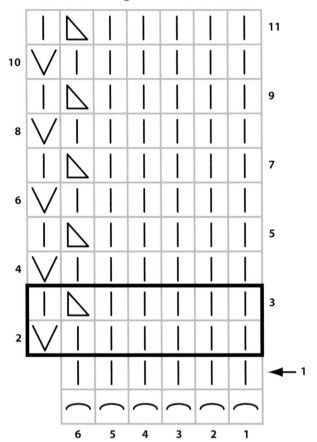

6-st RS Rectangles (repeat across work)—Chart 2B

Working down the slanted edge of the base triangle upon which you've just built the Right Edge triangle, work a RS Rectangle as foll:

Row 1 (RS): PU&K 6 sts evenly spaced along the left edge of the base triangle.

Row 2: Sl 1, p5, turn work.

Row 3: K5, k2tog-L, turn work.

Rep Rows 2–3 four times more, until no sts rem to be decreased into on the right edge of the base triangle.

Cont in the same manner, create 15 (17, 19, 21) full rectangles between the base triangles. There should be one left edge of the last base triangle rem to be worked.

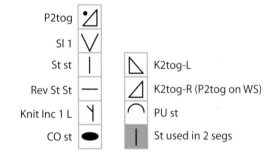

P2tog	⚊
Sl 1	V
St st		
Rev St St	—
Knit Inc 1 L	Y
CO st	●

K2tog-L	◺
K2tog-R (P2tog on WS)	◿
PU st	⌒
St used in 2 segs		

Chart 2C
Ending Triangle

Note: Button band sts are not shown.

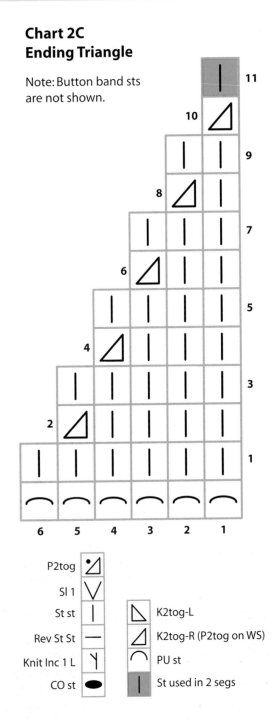

	Symbol
P2tog	◺•
Sl 1	V
St st	│
Rev St St	—
Knit Inc 1 L	Y
CO st	⬤
K2tog-L	◸
K2tog-R (P2tog on WS)	◹
PU st	⌒
St used in 2 segs	▮

6-st Left Edge Triangle (make one at end of band)—Chart 2C

Working down the slanted edge of the final base triangle:
Row 1 (RS): PU&K 6 sts evenly spaced along the left edge of the base triangle, sm, k5 button band sts.
Row 2 (WS): K5, p2tog, p4.
Row 3: K10.
Row 4: K5, p2tog, p3.
Row 5: K5, k2tog-R, yo, k2 (buttonhole row).
Row 6: K5, p2tog, p2.
Row 7: K8.
Row 8: K5, p2tog, p1.
Row 9: K7.

Row 10: K5, p2tog. The last st rem of triangle will become the first st of the first rectangle in the next band on the needle.

BAND THREE
7-st WS Rectangles

Working down the slanted edge of the second band rectangle upon which you've just built the Left Edge triangle, work a WS Rectangle as foll:
Row 1 (WS): PU&P 7 sts evenly spaced along the left edge of the rectangle from the prev band (using the last st from the prev band end triangle in the first rectangle only).
Row 2 (RS): Sl 1, k6, turn work.
Row 3: P6, p2tog-tbl, turn work.
Rep Rows 2–3 five times more, until no sts rem to be decreased into on the right edge of the base triangle.
Cont in the same manner, create 16 (18, 20, 22) full rectangles.

BAND FOUR
7-st Right Edge Triangle

Turn work so RS is facing, k5, sm.
Row 1 (RS): K2.
Row 2 (WS): P2.
Row 3: Kfb (increase of one st), k2tog-L.
Row 4: Sl 1, p2.
Row 5: Kfb, k1, k2tog-L.
Continue working as est until all sts in the last rectangle from the prev band have been decreased, and there are 7 sts in the Right Edge Triangle.

7-st Rectangles

Working down the slanted edge of the base triangle upon which you've just built the Right Edge triangle, work a RS Rectangle as foll:
Row 1 (RS): PU&K 7 sts evenly spaced along the left edge of the base triangle.
Row 2: Sl 1, p6, turn work.
Row 3: K6, k2tog-L, turn work.
Rep Rows 2–3 until no sts rem to be decreased into on the right edge of the previous band's rectangle.
Cont in the same manner, create 15 (17, 19, 21) full rectangles between the last band of rectangles.

7-st Left Edge Triangle

Working down the slanted edge of the final rectangle from the prev band:
Row 1 (RS): PU&K 7 sts evenly spaced along the left edge of the final rectangle from the prev band, sm, k5 button band sts.
Row 2 (WS): K5, p2tog, p5.
Row 3: K11.
Row 4: K5, p2tog, p4.
Row 5: K6, k2tog-R, yo, k2 (buttonhole row).
Row 6: K5, p2tog, p3.
Row 7: K9.

Cont in the same manner (with no further buttonhole in this triangle) until only 6 sts rem (5 edge sts + 1). End with a RS row.

BAND FIVE
8-st WS Rectangles

Working down the slanted edge of the fourth band rectangle upon which you've just built the Left Edge triangle, work a WS Rectangle as foll:

Row 1 (WS): PU&P 8 sts evenly spaced along the left edge of the rectangle from the prev band (using the last st from the prev band end triangle in the first rectangle only).

Row 2 (RS): Sl 1, k7, turn work.

Row 3: P7, p2tog-tbl, turn work.

Rep Rows 2–3 until no sts rem to be decreased into on the right edge of the base triangle.

Cont in the same manner, create 16 (18, 20, 22) full rectangles.

BAND SIX
7-st Right Edge Triangle

Turn work so RS is facing, k5, sm.

Row 1 (RS): K2.

Row 2 (WS): P2.

Row 3: Kfb (increase of one st), k2tog-L.

Row 4: Sl 1, p2.

Row 5: Kfb, k1, k2tog-L

Continue working as est until all sts in the last rectangle from the prev band have been decreased, and there are 7 sts in the Right Edge Triangle.

8-st Rectangles

Working down the slanted edge of the base triangle upon which you've just built the Right Edge triangle, work a RS Rectangle as foll:

Row 1 (RS): PU&K 8 sts evenly spaced along the left edge of the base triangle.

Row 2: Sl 1, p7, turn work.

Row 3: K7, k2tog-L, turn work.

Rep Rows 2–3 until no sts rem to be decreased into on the right edge of the previous band's rectangle.

Cont in the same manner, create 15 (17, 19, 21) full rectangles between the last band of rectangles.

8-st Left Edge Triangle

Working down the slanted edge of the final rectangle from the prev band:

Row 1 (RS): PU&K 8 sts evenly spaced along the left edge of the final rectangle from the prev band, sm, k5 button band sts.

Row 2 (WS): K5, p2tog, p6.

Row 3: K12.

Row 4: K5, p2tog, p5.

Row 5: K7, k2tog-R, yo, k2 (buttonhole row).

Row 6: K5, p2tog, p4.

Row 7: K10.

Cont in the same manner (with no further buttonhole in this triangle) until only 5 sts rem (5 edge sts +1). End with a RS row.

BAND SEVEN
9-st WS Rectangles

Working down the slanted edge of the sixth band rectangle upon which you've just built the Left Edge triangle, work a WS Rectangle as foll:

Row 1 (WS): PU&P 9 sts evenly spaced along the left edge of the rectangle from the prev band (using the last st from the prev band end triangle in the first rectangle only).

Row 2 (RS): Sl 1, k8, turn work.

Row 3: P8, p2tog-tbl, turn work.

Rep Rows 2–3 until no sts rem to be decreased into on the right edge of the base triangle.

Cont in the same manner, create 16 (18, 20, 22) full rectangles.

BAND EIGHT
9-st Right Edge Triangle

Turn work so RS is facing, k5, sm.

Row 1 (RS): K2.

Row 2 (WS): P2.

Row 3: Kfb (increase of one st), k2tog-L.

Row 4: Sl 1, p2.

Row 5: Kfb, k1, k2tog-L.

Continue working as est until all sts in the last rectangle from the prev band have been decreased, and there are 9 sts in the Right Edge Triangle.

9-st Rectangles

Working down the slanted edge of the base triangle upon which you've just built the Right Edge triangle, work a RS Rectangle as foll:

Row 1 (RS): PU&K 9 sts evenly spaced along the left edge of the base triangle.

Row 2: Sl 1, p8, turn work.

Row 3: K8, k2tog-L, turn work.

Rep Rows 2–3 until no sts rem to be decreased into on the right edge of the previous band's rectangle.

Cont in the same manner, create 15 (17, 19, 21) full rectangles between the last band of rectangles.

9-st Left Edge Triangle

Working down the slanted edge of the final rectangle from the prev band.

Row 1 (RS): PU&K 9 sts evenly spaced along the left edge of the final rectangle from the prev band, sm, k5 button band sts.

Row 2 (WS): K5, p2tog, p7.

Row 3: K13.

Row 4: K5, p2tog, p6.

Row 5: K8, k2tog-R, yo, k2 (buttonhole row).

Row 6: K5, p2tog, p5.

Row 7: K11.

Cont in the same manner (with no further buttonhole in this triangle) until only 5 sts rem (5 edge sts +1), ending with a RS row.

BAND NINE
10-st WS Rectangles

Working down the slanted edge of the eighth band rectangle upon which you've just built the Left Edge triangle, work a WS Rectangle as foll:

Row 1 (WS): PU&P 10 sts evenly spaced along the left edge of the rectangle from the prev band (using the last st from the prev band end triangle in the first rectangle only).

Row 2 (RS): Sl 1, k9, turn work.

Row 3: P9, p2tog-tbl, turn work.

Rep Rows 2–3 until no sts rem to be decreased into on the right edge of the base triangle.

Cont in the same manner, create 16 (18, 20, 22) full rectangles.

BAND TEN
11-st Right Edge Triangle

Turn work so RS is facing, k5, sm.

Row 1 (RS): K2.

Row 2 (WS): P2.

Row 3: Kfb (increase of one st), k2tog-L.

Row 4: Sl 1, p2.

Row 5: Kfb, k1, k2tog-L.

Continue working as est until all sts in the last rectangle from the prev band have been decreased, and there are 11 sts in the Right Edge Triangle.

11-st Rectangles

Working down the slanted edge of the base triangle upon which you've just built the Right Edge triangle, work a RS Rectangle as foll:

Row 1 (RS): PU&K 11 sts evenly spaced along the left edge of the base triangle.

Row 2: Sl 1, p10, turn work.

Row 3: K10, k2tog-L, turn work.

Rep Rows 2–3 until no sts rem to be decreased into on the right edge of the previous band's rectangle.

Cont in the same manner, create 15 (17, 19, 21) full rectangles between the last band of rectangles.

11-st Left Edge Triangle

Working down the slanted edge of the final rectangle from the prev band:

Row 1 (RS): PU&K 11 sts evenly spaced along the left edge of the final rectangle from the prev band, sm, k5 button band sts.

Row 2 (WS): K5, p2tog, p9.

Row 3: K15.

Row 4: K5, p2tog, p8.

Row 5: K10, k2tog-R, yo, k2 (buttonhole row).

Row 6: K5, p2tog, p7.

Row 7: K13.

Cont in the same manner (with no further buttonhole in this triangle) until only 6 sts rem (5 edge sts +1). End with a RS row.

BAND ELEVEN
12-st RS Rectangles

Working down the slanted edge of the fourth band rectangle upon which you've just built the Left Edge triangle, work a WS Rectangle as foll:

Row 1 (WS): PU&P 12 sts evenly spaced along the left edge of the rectangle from the prev band (using the last st from the prev band end triangle in the first rectangle only).

Row 2 (RS): Sl 1, k11, turn work.

Row 3: P11, p2tog-tbl, turn work.

Rep Rows 2–3 until no sts rem to be decreased into on the right edge of the base triangle.

Cont in the same manner, create 16 (18, 20, 22) full rectangles.

BAND TWELVE
13-st Right Edge Triangle

Turn work so RS is facing, k5, sm.

Row 1 (RS): K2.

Row 2 (WS): P2.

Row 3: Kfb (increase of one st), k2tog-L.

Row 4: Sl 1, p2.
Row 5: Kfb, k1, k2tog-L.
Continue working as est until all sts in the last rectangle from the prev band have been decreased, and there are 13 sts in the Right Edge Triangle.

13-st Rectangles

Working down the slanted edge of the base triangle upon which you've just built the Right Edge triangle, work a RS Rectangle as foll:
Row 1 (RS): PU&K 13 sts evenly spaced along the left edge of the base triangle.
Row 2: Sl 1, p12, turn work.
Row 3: K12, k2tog-L, turn work.
Rep Rows 2–3 until no sts rem to be decreased into on the right edge of the previous band's rectangle.
Cont in the same manner, create 15 (17, 19, 21) full rectangles between the last band of rectangles.

13-st Left Edge Triangle

Working down the slanted edge of the final rectangle from the prev band:
Row 1 (RS): PU&K 13 sts evenly spaced along the left edge of the final rectangle from the prev band, sm, k5 button band sts.
Row 2 (WS): K5, p2 tog, p11.
Row 3: K17.
Row 4: K5, p2tog, p10.
Row 5: K12, k2tog-R, yo, k2 (buttonhole row).
Row 6: K5, p2tog, p9.
Row 7: K15.
Cont in the same manner (with no further buttonhole in this triangle) until only 6 sts rem (5 edge sts +1). End with a RS row.

BAND THIRTEEN
14-st RS Rectangles

Working down the slanted edge of the twelfth band rectangle upon which you've just built the Left Edge triangle, work a WS Rectangle as foll:
Row 1 (WS): PU&P 14 sts evenly spaced along the left edge of the rectangle from the prev band (using the last st from the prev band end triangle in the first rectangle only).
Row 2 (RS): Sl 1, k13, turn work.
Row 3: P13, p2tog-tbl, turn work.
Rep Rows 2–3 until no sts rem to be decreased into on the right edge of the base triangle.
Cont in the same manner, create 16 (18, 20, 22) full rectangles.

BAND FOURTEEN
14-st Right Edge Final Triangle—Chart 3A

Turn work so RS is facing, k5, sm.
Row 1 (RS): Kfb, k2tog-L.
Row 2 and all WS rows: Sl 1, purl to the last 5 sts, k5.
Row 3: K2, k2tog-L.

Row 5: Kfb, k1, k2tog-L.
Row 7: K3, k2tog-L.
Row 9: Kfb, k2, k2tog-L.
Row 11: K4, k2tog-L.
Row 13: Kfb, k3, k2tog-L.
Row 15: K5, k2tog-L.
Row 17: Kfb, k4, k2tog-L.
Row 19: K6, k2tog-L.
Row 21: Kfb, k5, k2tog-L.
Row 23: K7, k2tog-L—8 sts rem on RH needle.

Chart 3A
Final Beginning Triangle

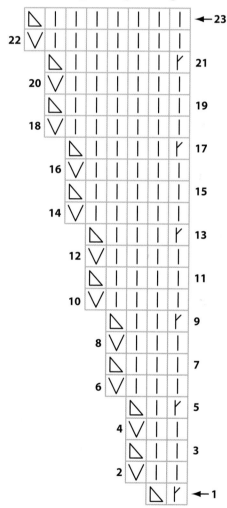

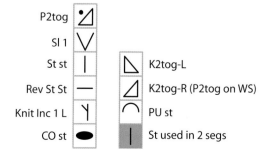

14-st Center Final Triangles—Chart 3B

Working down the slanted edge of the base triangle upon which you've just built the Right Edge triangle, work a RS triangle as foll:

Row 1 (RS): PU&K 14 sts evenly spaced along the left edge of the base triangle.
Row 2: Sl 1, p13, turn work.
Row 3: K2tog-L, k12, k2tog-L.
Row 4 and all WS rows: Sl 1, p to end of row, turn work.
Row 5: K2tog-L, k11, k2tog-L.
Row 7: K2tog-L, k10, k2tog-L.
Row 9: K2tog-L, k9, k2tog-L.
Row 11: K2tog-L, k8, k2tog-L.
Row 13: K2tog-L, k7, k2tog-L.
Row 15: K2tog-L, k6, k2tog-L.
Row 17: K2tog-L, k5, k2tog-L.
Row 19: K2tog-L, k4, k2tog-L.
Row 21: K2tog-L, k3, k2tog-L.
Row 23: K2tog-L, k2, k2tog-L.
Row 25: K2tog-L, k1, k2tog-L.
Row 27: K2tog-L, k1.

Row 29: K2tog-L. (Do not tie off this st, use it as the first PU st of next triangle).
Cont in the same manner, create 15 (17, 19, 21) final triangles between the last band of rectangles.

14-st Left Edge Final Triangle—Chart 3C

Working down the slanted edge of the final rectangle from the prev band:

Row 1 (RS): PU&K 14 sts evenly spaced along the left edge of the final rectangle from the prev band, sm, k5 button band sts.
Row 2 (WS): K5, p2tog, p10, p2tog.
Row 3: K17.
Row 4: K5, p2tog, p8, p2tog.
Row 5: K11, k2tog-R, yo, k2 (buttonhole row).
Row 6: K5, p2tog, p6, p2tog.
Row 7: K13.
Row 8: K5, p2tog, p4, p2tog.
Row 9: K11.
Row 10: K5, p2tog, p2, p2tog.
Row 11: K9.
Row 12: K5, p2tog twice.
Row 13: K2.
Row 14: P2tog.

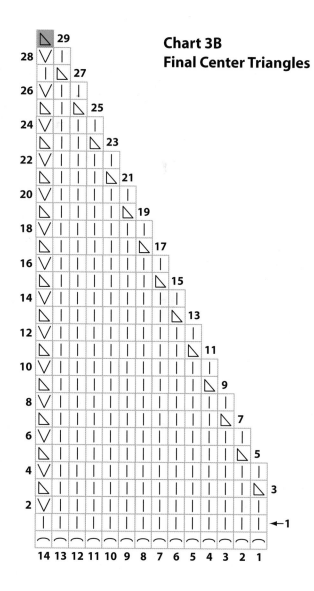

**Chart 3B
Final Center Triangles**

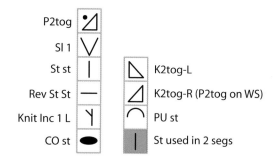

P2tog	⊡
Sl 1	V
St st	│
Rev St St	—
Knit Inc 1 L	Y
CO st	●

K2tog-L	◸
K2tog-R (P2tog on WS)	◿
PU st	⌒
St used in 2 segs	▊

Chart 3C
Final Ending Triangle

Note: Button band sts are not shown.

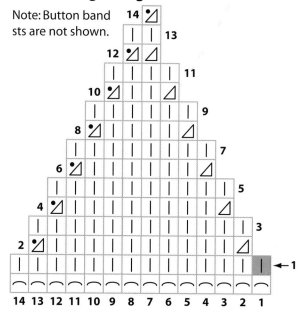

Neck

Return to provisionally cast-on sts and slip them carefully onto needle. Choose a portion of the ball of yarn that merges gracefully with the beginning rows of the poncho.

Row 1 (RS): [K3, k2tog] 21 (23, 26, 28) times—85 (95, 104, 114) sts

Row 2 (WS): Knit all sts, dec 1 (3, 0, 2) sts evenly across work—84 (92, 104, 112) sts.

ESTABLISH DKSS EDGES AND RIBBING

Row 3: {K1, wyrs sl 1, k1}, [p2, k2] rep to last 5 sts, p2, {k1, wyrs sl 1, k1}.

Row 4: {Wyws sl 1, k1, wyws sl 1}, work in rib as est to last 3 sts, {wyws sl 1, k1, wyws sl 1}.

Rep last 2 rows until neck meas 3"/7.5 cm or desired length. End with a WS row.

Next row (RS): Work I-cord BO across all sts as follows.

To start, cast on 3 sts at start of row.

1. K2, k2tog-L.
2. Slip 3 sts from RH needle back onto LH needle.
3. Pull yarn taut across back of work.
4. Repeat steps 1–3 across work until 3 sts rem.
5. End k3tog-L, tie off last stitch.

Finishing

With a yarn needle, weave in ends. Steam block piece.

Using yarn that matches the area of the button band where each hole is formed, create seven crocheted buttons (or use purchased ones), as described below, and stitch in place on the Left Garter Band to match the buttonhole placements on the Right Garter Band.

CROCHETED BUTTON

With a single strand of yarn and size F-5 (3.75 mm) crochet hook and leaving a 12" tail, chain 4, join with a slip stitch to form ring.

Rnd 1: 12 sc into ring.

Rnd 2: [2 sc in next st] rep to end of rnd—24 sc.

Rnd 3: [1 sc, 2 sc in next st] rep to end of rnd—36 sc.

Rnd 4: [1 sc, skip 1] rep to end of rnd—18 sc.

Rnd 5: Rep Rnd 4—9 sc.

Measure 18" of yarn from the last stitch, break thread. Draw tail from chain into button and use it as filling to pad out the button. Thread yarn through remaining 9 sts and pull tight. Secure with a knot. Thread tail onto darning needle and push from back to front of button, then push back through to back of button catching one stitch, thus drawing the front and back of button together. Use remaining tail to secure button to garment.

Finished Measurements

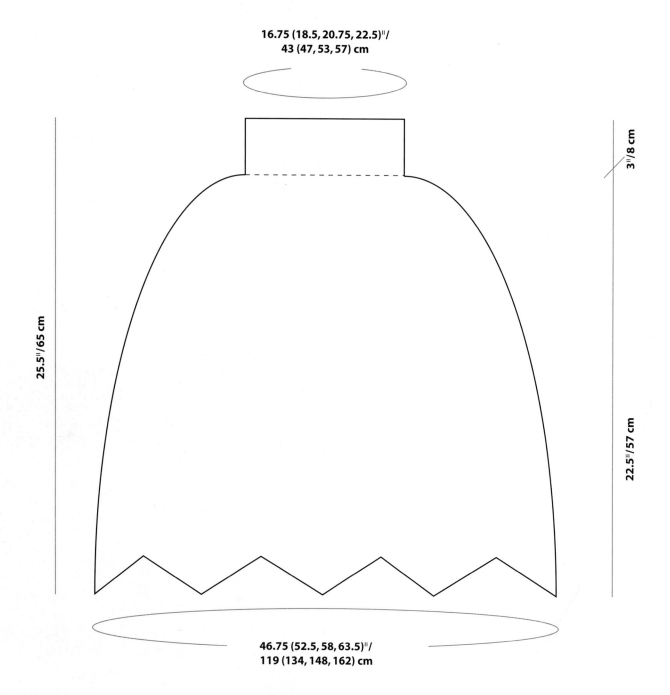

16.75 (18.5, 20.75, 22.5)"/
43 (47, 53, 57) cm

3"/8 cm

25.5"/65 cm

22.5"/57 cm

46.75 (52.5, 58, 63.5)"/
119 (134, 148, 162) cm

Fitted Lace Off-Shoulder Top

L ightweight, ethereal, almost elfin, this can be a transformative top. A soft, subtle, and body-conscious design, this lovely garment is meant to complement a simple tank or camisole, elevating it to an elegant place.

Finished Measurements

Bust: 32 (36, 40, 44)"/81.5 (92, 102, 112) cm
Length: $12^1/_2$ ($12^3/_4$, 14, 15)"/32 (32.5, 35.5, 38.5) cm

Skill Level

Intermediate

Yarn

Artyarns Ensemble Glitter Light, light weight #3 yarn (50% silk, 50% cashmere with Lurex; 400 yd./365 m per 2.8 oz./80 g skein)
- 2 (3, 3, 4) skeins #308 Cream

Needles and Other Materials

- US 5 (3.75 mm) needles
- US D-3 (3.25 mm) crochet hook
- Yarn needle
- Nine 2 mm bead buttons
- Waste yarn
- Sewing needle and matching thread

Gauge

20 sts x 36 rows in Lace patt = 4"/10 cm square
Adjust needle size if necessary to obtain gauge.

Stitches & Techniques

Ch (chain)
Form a slipknot and place on hook. Yarn over hook. Pull yarn through slipknot (one loop on hook; one chain made). [Yarn over hook, pull yarn through loop on hook] rep until desired number of chain sts are formed.

K2tog-L (knit 2 tog with a left slant)
Knit 2 stitches together so the working needle is pointing to the left as it enters the stitch (dec will slant to the left); common left-slanting decreases are ssk, k2tog-tbl, or skp.

K2tog-R (knit 2 tog with a right slant)
Knit 2 stitches together so the working needle is pointing to the right as it enters the stitch (dec will slant to the right); most common is k2tog.

Sc (single crochet)
Insert hook in stitch. Yarn over hook. Pull yarn through stitch. Yarn over hook. Pull yarn through 2 loops on hook (one single crochet made).

Body

CO 160 (180, 200, 220) sts, pm to note start of round.
Next rnd: [K1, p2, k1] rep around work 40 (45, 50, 55) times. Cont working in rib as est until work meas 1"/2.5 cm from CO.

BEGIN LACE PATTERN

Rnd 1: Work in rib as est for 40 (40, 40, 50) sts, pm, work Row 1 of chart across next 40 (50, 60, 60) sts, pm, work 80 (90, 100, 110) sts to end of round.
Next rnd: Cont working in rib as est, working lace chart between markers.
Rep last round until all 24 rows of lace chart have been worked, remove marker at start of round, break yarn.

Fitted Lace Off-Shoulder Top Chart

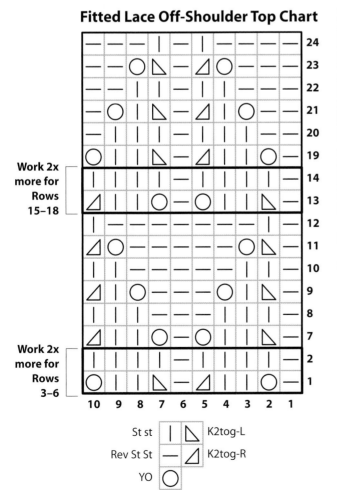

Work 2x more for Rows 15–18

Work 2x more for Rows 3–6

St st	❘
Rev St st	—
YO	○
K2tog-L	◣
K2tog-R	◢

Fitted Lace Off-Shoulder Chart Written Instructions—Worked in the Round, RS Only

Rnd 1: [P1, yo, k2, k2tog-R, p1, k2tog-L, k2, yo] rep around work.

Rnd 2: [(P1, k4) twice] rep around work.

Rnds 3–6: Rep Rnds 1–2 twice more.

Rnd 7: [P1, k2tog-L, k2, yo, p1, yo, k2, k2tog-R] rep around work.

Rnd 8: [P1, k3, p3, k3] rep around work.

Rnd 9: [P1, k2tog-L, k1, yo, p3, yo, k1, k2tog-R] rep around work.

Rnd 10: [P1, k2, p5, k2] rep around work.

Rnd 11: [P1, k2tog-L, yo, p5, yo, k2tog-R] rep around work.

Rnd 12: [P1, k1, p7, k1] rep around work.

Rnd 13: [P1, k2tog-L, k2, yo, p1, yo, k2, k2tog-R] rep around work.

Rnd 14: [(P1, k4) twice] rep around work.

Rnds 15–18: Rep Rnds 13–14 twice more.

Rnd 19: [P1, yo, k2, k2tog-R, p1, k2tog-L, k2, yo] rep around work.

Rnd 20: [P2, k3, p1, k3, p1] rep around work.

Rnd 21: [P2, yo, k1, k2tog-R, p1, k2tog-L, k1, yo, p1] rep around work.

Rnd 22: [P3, k2, p1, k2, p2] rep around work.

Rnd 23: [P3, yo, k2tog-R, p1, k2tog-L, yo, p2] rep around work.

Rnd 24: [P4, k1, p1, k1, p3] rep around work.

Fitted Lace Off-Shoulder Chart Written Instructions—Worked Back and Forth, RS and WS

Row 1 (RS): [P1, yo, k2, k2tog-R, p1, k2tog-L, k2, yo] rep across work.

Row 2 (WS): [(P4, k1) twice] rep across work.

Rows 3–6: Rep Rows 1–2 twice more.

Row 7: [P1, k2tog-L, k2, yo, p1, yo, k2, k2tog-R] rep across work.

Row 8: [P3, k3, p3, k1] rep across work.

Row 9: [P1, k2tog-L, k1, yo, p3, yo, k1, k2tog-R] rep across work.

Row 10: [P2, k5, p2, k1] rep across work.

Row 11: [P1, k2tog-L, yo, p5, yo, k2tog-R] rep across work.

Row 12: [P1, k7, p1, k1] rep across work.

Row 13: [P1, K2tog-L, k2, yo, p1, yo, k2, k2tog-R] rep across work.

Row 14: [(P4, k1) twice] rep across work.

Row 15–18: Rep Rows 13–14 twice more.

Row 19: [P1, yo, k2, k2tog-R, p1, k2tog-L, k2, yo] rep across work.

Row 20: [K1, p3, k1, p3, k2] rep across work.

Row 21: [P2, yo, k1, k2tog-R, p1, k2tog-L, k1, yo, p1] rep across work.

Row 22: [K2, p2, k1, p2, k3] rep across work.

Row 23: [P3, yo, k2tog-R, p1, k2tog-L, yo, p2] rep across work.

Row 24: [K3, p1, k1, p1, k4] rep across work.

DIVIDE FRONT

Reorient stitches so that you are in the center of the lace pattern, 20 (25, 30, 30) sts in from each marker, this will be the point of the center front divide.

Row 1 (RS): Place contrasting marker to note center divide point. CO 1 st (edge st at right center front), p1 (first st in chart) cont in lace patt as est to next marker, work 80 (90, 100, 110) sts in rib as est to next marker, work in lace patt as est across 20 (25, 30, 30) sts to contrasting marker, CO 2 sts at end of row—163 (183, 203, 223) sts.

Row 2 (WS): Sl 1, k1, cont in lace patt as est to marker, work in rib as est to next marker, work in lace patt as est to last 2 sts, end k2.

Row 3 (RS): Sl 1, work in lace patt as est to marker, work in rib to next marker, work in lace patt to 2 sts before end of row, end p1, k1.

Row 4 (WS): Sl 1, k1, work in lace patt as est to marker, work in rib to next marker, work in lace patt to 2 st before end of row, end p1, k1.

Rep last 2 rows until work meas 7$\frac{1}{2}$ (7$\frac{1}{2}$, 8, 8)"/19 (19, 20.5, 20.5) cm from CO edge.

DIVIDE FOR ARMHOLES

Work 40 (45, 50, 55) sts in lace and rib patt as est, work next 80 (90, 100, 110) sts in rib as est and slip these 80 (90, 100, 110) back sts to holder to work later. Join second ball of yarn and work rem 40 (45, 50, 55) sts in rib and lace patt as est.

Fronts

Working both Fronts together at the same time using a separate ball of yarn for each, cont working in Lace and Rib patts as est while *at the same time* dec 1 st at each armhole edge every other row 10 (11, 12, 13) times—30 (34, 38, 42) sts rem at each front.

Cont in lace and rib patts as est, work even with no further decreasing until piece meas 3$\frac{1}{2}$ (3$\frac{3}{4}$, 4$\frac{1}{2}$, 5$\frac{1}{2}$)"/9 (9.5, 11.5, 14) cm from armhole divide. Slip sts onto holder to work later.

Back

Return to Back sts on holder and slide them onto needle. Continue working in rib as est, decreasing 1 st at each edge every other row 10 (11, 12, 13) times, until 60 (68, 76, 84) sts rem. Work even until length is same as Fronts.

JOINING FRONTS TO BACK

Next row (RS): Cont with a single ball of yarn and beginning with Right Front, work in lace patt as est across all 30 (34, 38, 42) sts (including rib sts), with a separate piece of waste yarn provisionally CO 20 (26, 32, 28) upper Right Sleeve sts, work in rib as est across 60 (68, 76, 84) Back sts, with a second strand of waste yarn provisionally CO 20 (26, 32, 28) upper Left Sleeve sts, beg at armhole edge of Left Front work in rib and lace patt as est—160 (188, 216, 224) Yoke sts total. (See page 118 for instructions on provisional CO.)

Next row (WS): Work in lace patt as est across Left Front and on across newly cast on Left Sleeve sts. Work in rib across Back sts as est, return to lace patt for Right Sleeve and across the Right Front.

Cont in lace and rib as est with no increasing or decreasing for at least 6 rows. Work to row 8 or 16 of charted patt.

Next row (RS): P3, [k2, p2] rep to last 3 sts, end p3.

Cont in rib as est for 6 rows. Bind off all sts loosely in rib.

Sleeve (Make 2)

Return to provisionally CO sts and slip onto circ needle. With RS facing, PU 36 (38, 48, 56) sts around bottom of armhole edge (along Front and Back decrease)—56 (64, 80, 84) sts, place marker to note start of round.

Work in k2, p2 rib for 5"/12.5 cm. Bind off all sts loosely in rib.

Front Placket

Row 1: With a size F-5 (3.75 mm) crochet hook sc 60 (66, 72, 78) down the left front edge from neck to point where Fronts join at waist. Cont up right front, sc 60 (66, 72, 78) to neck edge.

Row 2: Work 1 sc into each sc down right front and back up left front.

Row 3: Sc 60 (66, 72, 78) to bottom of left front, working up right front create 6 (3, 9, 6) buttonholes as foll: Sc 3 (1, 4, 3), [ch 3, sk 1 sc, sc 8] 6 (3, 9, 6) times, sc 3 (2, 5, 3) to right front neck edge. Tie off last st.

Finishing

Weave in ends. Steam block garment. Pin fronts together and sew a bead button on the left front to match the placement of each 3-ch button loop on the right front.

Finished Measurements

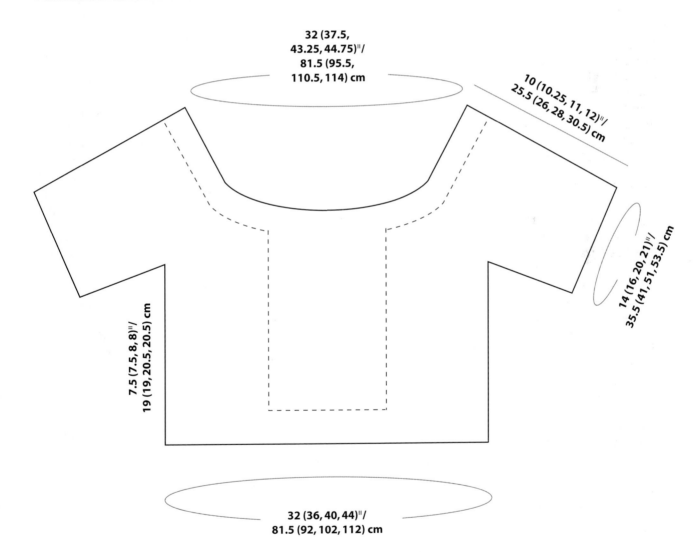

32 (37.5, 43.25, 44.75)"/ 81.5 (95.5, 110.5, 114) cm

10 (10.25, 11, 12)"/ 25.5 (26, 28, 30.5) cm

14 (16, 20, 21)"/ 35.5 (41, 51, 53.5) cm

7.5 (7.5, 8, 8)"/ 19 (19, 20.5, 20.5) cm

32 (36, 40, 44)"/ 81.5 (92, 102, 112) cm

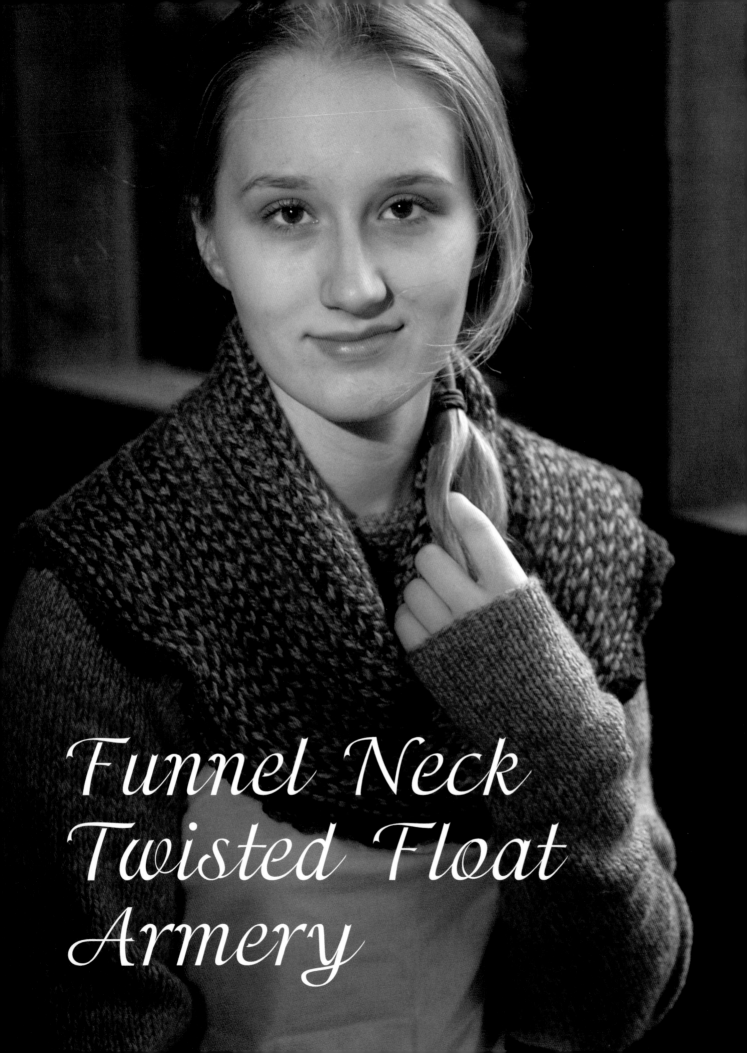

Funnel Neck
Twisted Float
Armery

This piece features a beautiful "wrong side" fabric of twisted floats, which has become one of my favorite ways to blend colors into a unique fabric.

The sleeves are knitted separately, then joined as the funnel neck is formed, creating a dramatic answer to the woman who wonders, "How can I keep my arms and neck warm?"

Sizes

To fit bust 30 (36, 42, 48, 54)"/76.5 (92, 107, 122.5, 138) cm

Finished Measurements

Sleeve length: 26 (27, 28, 29, 30)"/66.5 (69, 71.5, 74, 76.5) cm
Upper arm: 19^1/$_2$ (20^1/$_2$, 21, 22, 22^1/$_2$)"/49.5 (52.5, 53.5, 56, 57.5) cm

Skill Level

Intermediate

Yarn

Lorna's Laces Masham Worsted, medium weight #4 yarn (100% wool; 170 yd./155 m per 3.5 oz./100 g ball)
- 3 (4, 6, 7, 8) balls Watercolor (Color A)
- 2 (3, 4, 5, 6) balls Old Rose (Color B)

Needles and Other Materials

- US 7 (4.5 mm) circular needle
- 8 stitch markers
- Waste yarn

Gauge

17 sts x 22 rows in Twisted Float patt = 4"/10 cm square
Adjust needle size if necessary to obtain gauge.

Stitch Guide

Cable Cast-On

Slip needle between first and second sts on LH needle and pull loop through to front. Slip this loop onto the LH needle twisting it clockwise (in other words, "back" the stitch onto the left needle). Repeat, each time using newly created st as first stitch on LH needle.

Dkss Edge (double knit slipped st edge, worked over 3 sts)

This edging is created by slipping and knitting stitches, keeping in mind that whenever stitches are slipped at either 3-st edge, the yarn is held *toward* the knitter, regardless of whether the right or wrong side is facing the knitter. On the RS rows, at either end, the 3 edge sts are worked knit, slip, knit. On the WS rows, at either end, the 3 edge sts are worked slip, knit, slip.

RS Row: {K1, wyrs sl 1, k1}, work to last 3 sts, {k1, wyrs sl 1, k1}.
WS Row: {Wyws sl 1, k1, wyws sl 1}, work to last 3 sts, {wyws sl 1, k1, wyws sl 1}.

K3tog-L (knit 3 tog with a left slant)

Knit 3 sts together so the working needle is pointing to the left as it enters the stitch (dec will slant to the left); common decreases are sssk, k3togTBL, or sl2, k1, psso.

K3tog-R (knit 3 tog with a right slant)

Knit 3 sts together so the working needle is pointing to the right as it enters the stitch (dec will slant to the right); most common is k3tog.

Kfb (knit into front and back of same stitch)

Knit into the front and back of one stitch, then kick that stitch off the needle—increase of 1 st.

Wyrs sl 1 (with yarn right side, slip 1)

Move yarn to RS of work. Insert RH needle purlwise into st and slip off of LH needle.

Wyws sl 1 (with yarn wrong side, slip 1)

Move yarn to WS of work. Insert RH needle purlwise into st and slip off of LH needle.

Sleeve (Make 2)

With A and circ needle, CO 32 (34, 36, 40, 44) sts. Place marker to note start of round.
Work in St st (knit every round) for 4 rounds.

SLEEVE SHAPING

Next Round: K1, kfb, k to 2 sts before marker, kfb, k1—34 (36, 38, 42, 46) sts.
Next 5 Rounds: Knit all sts.
Work the last 6 rounds 23 (24, 24, 24, 23) total times—78 (82, 84, 88, 90) sts total. Work even with no further increasing until sleeve meas 26 (27, 28, 29, 30)"/66.5 (69, 71.5, 74, 76.5) cm from cast-on edge.

ARMHOLE SHAPING

Begin working back and forth in rows.
Row 1: {K1, wyrs sl 1, k1}, p2, k to last 5 sts, p2, {k1, wyrs sl 1, k1}.
Row 2: {Wyws sl 1, k1, wyws sl 1}, k2, p to last 5 sts, k2, {wyws sl 1, k1, wyws sl 1}.
Rep Rows 1–2 5 (6, 7, 8, 10) times—10 (12, 14, 16, 20) rows total.

Next row: {Dkss RS edge}, p2, k3tog-L, k to last 8 sts, k3tog-R, p2, {dkss RS edge}—74 (78, 80, 84, 86) sts.
Next row: {Dkss WS edge}, k2, p to last 5 sts, k2, {dkss WS edge}.
Rep Rows 3–4 14 (14, 14, 15, 15) times more until 18 (22, 24, 24, 26) sts rem. Work even with no further decreasing until sleeve depth meas 9^1/$_2$ (10, 10^1/$_2$, 11^1/$_2$, 12^1/$_2$)"/ 24 (25.5, 27, 29.5, 32) cm. Slip sts onto a piece of waste yarn to work later.

Collar

Slip sts from both sleeves onto circ needle. With RS of sleeve facing and with A, knit across 18 (22, 24, 24, 26) sts of first sleeve.
Cable CO 22 (22, 24, 28, 30) sts, then knit across 18 (22, 24, 24, 26) sts of second sleeve. Cable CO 22 (22, 24, 28, 30) sts and join to work in round, placing a marker to note start of round—80 (88, 96, 104, 112) sts.
Next rnd: Purl all sts.
Next rnd: Join B, [K10 (11, 12, 13, 14) sts, pm] eight times.

BEGIN TWISTED FLOAT PATTERN

Following Funnel Neck Armery Chart, work Twisted Float patt as foll:

Rnd 1: *[With B, k1, drop strand of B. Bring strand of A *under* strand of B and with A, k1, drop strand of A. Bring strand of B *under* strand of A] rep to first marker, alternating between A and B and always bringing the new strand of yarn *under* the old strand. At marker, [reverse the direction of the strands, alternating between A and B and always bringing new strand *over* old strand] rep to next marker. Rep from * three times more, eight sections between eight markers in total.

Rnd 2: *[With B, k1, bring strand of A *over* strand of B and with A, k1, bring strand of B *over* strand of A and with A, k1] rep to first marker, alternating between A and B and always bringing the new strand of yarn *over* the old strand. At marker, [reverse the direction of the strands, alternating between A and B and always bringing new strand *under* old strand] rep to next marker. Rep from * three times more, eight sections between eight markers in total.

Rnd 3: With A, purl all sts.

Rnd 4: With B, knit all sts, inc 1 st in each section by working a kfb anywhere between markers—88 (96, 104, 112, 120) sts, being careful to stagger increase placement in subsequent rounds so they are not directly above each other.

Rep last 4 rnds 13 (14, 15, 16, 17) times, alternating the twists of the floats from marker to marker and from row to row, creating a herringbone pattern and increasing in each section every eighth row until there are 184 (200, 216, 232, 248) sts total in the collar.

PICOT BIND-OFF

Next rnd: With B, knit all sts.

Next rnd: With B, purl all sts.

Next rnd: Work a picot bind-off (see page 120 for photo-illustrated instructions), creating a 2-ch picot at each bound off stitch for a ruffled edge on the collar, as foll:
1. K2tog-L.
2. Slip the st created back onto the LH needle and knit it.
3. Slip the st just created back onto the LH needle and knit it.
4. Slip the stitch created back onto the LH needle and work it, together with the next st, as a k2tog-L.

Rep steps 2–4 around work until all sts are bound off.

Finishing

Weave in ends. Steam block piece.

Funnel Neck Armery

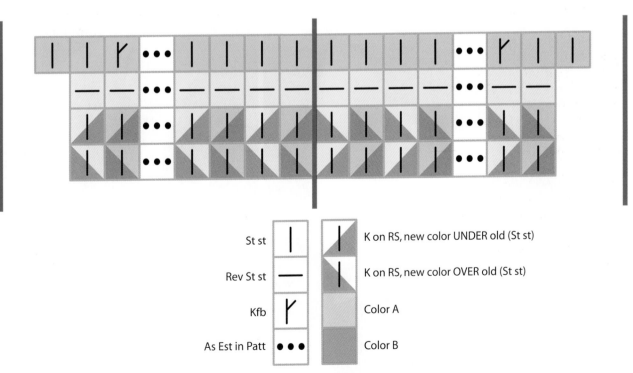

St st		K on RS, new color UNDER old (St st)
Rev St st		K on RS, new color OVER old (St st)
Kfb		Color A
As Est in Patt		Color B

Finished Measurements

50 (56, 60, 66, 70)"/
127.5 (143, 153,
168.5, 178.5) cm

9.5 (10, 10.5,
11.5, 12.5)"/
24 (25.5, 27,
29.5, 32) cm

15 (17, 18, 20, 21)"/
38.5 (43.5, 46, 51, 53.5) cm

26 (27, 28, 29, 30)"/66.5 (69, 71.5, 74, 76.5) cm

19.5 (20.5,
21, 22, 22.5)"/
49.5 (52.5, 53.5,
56, 57.5) cm

20 (22, 24,
26, 28)"/
51 (56, 61,
66.5, 71.5) cm

8 (8.5,
9, 10, 11)"/
20.5 (21.5, 23,
25.5, 28) cm

Log Cabin Cardigan

A square of smaller mitered squares is the origination point for this simple cardigan. Throughout the project, use a separate piece of waste yarn on either side of each square and "log" to catch the first stitch of each row. This will make picking up and knitting these caught stitches of yarn much easier in subsequent rows.

Sizes

One Size

Note: This is a one-size garment that will fit a variety of people well. If a larger garment is desired, either add more "logs" in the manner established, or increase the garter border surrounding the piece. If a smaller garment is desired, reduce the number of "logs" or decrease the rows in the garter border.

Finished Measurements

61"/155 cm square

Skill Level

Intermediate

Yarn

Brooklyn Tweed Shelter, medium weight #4 yarn (100% wool; 140 yd./128 m per 1.75 oz./50 g skein)
- 1 skein Almanac (Color A)
- 1 skein Pumpernickel (Color B)
- 1 skein Hayloft (Color C)
- 1 skein Tent (Color D)
- 2 skeins Long Johns (Color E)
- 1 skein Thistle (Color F)

Needles and Other Materials

- US 7 (4.5 mm) circular needles
- Optional: US G-6 (4 mm) crochet hook and shank button for closure

Gauge

18 sts x 36 rows in garter st = 4"/10 cm square
Adjust needle size if necessary to obtain gauge.

Stitch Guide

PU (pick up)

Using the knitting needle only, with no source of yarn, pick up a loop from the existing fabric to create a stitch on the needle.

PU&K (pick up & knit)

Insert needle into next stitch, stabbing all the way from the right side to the wrong side of the work. Wrap a loop around the needle, pull the loop through, creating a knit stitch.

VDD (vertical double decrease)

Sl 2 sts as if to work k2tog-R, k1, pass slipped sts over—decrease of 2 sts.

Tip for Picking Up Stitches

As you work each log, use a separate piece of waste yarn on either side of each square and log to catch the first stitch of each row. This will make picking up these caught loops of yarn much easier in subsequent rows. When picking up sts, use a circular needle to make arrangement of stitches for working easier.

1. Here you can see previously caught stitches on the waste yarn.

2. When you begin the first stitch of the row, catch the waste yarn behind the stitch.

3. Wrap the waste yarn.

4. Knit the stitch.

5. The waste yarn is caught and will help you to find the correct loop to pick up when needed.

9-Square Center Mitered Section

Log Cabin Cardigan Schematic

North

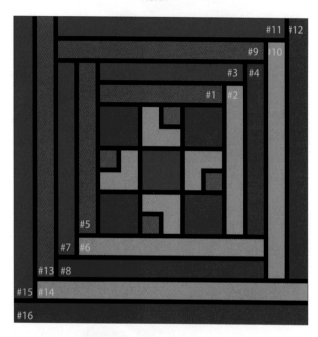

Log Cabin Center Square

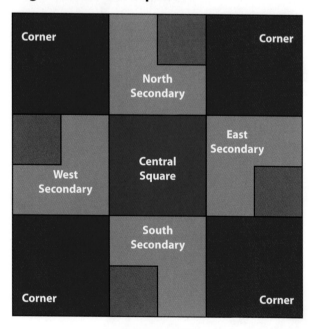

CENTRAL SQUARE

With A and a piece of waste yarn, provisionally CO 12 sts. (See page 118 for how to work a provisional cast-on.)
Work 24 rows in garter, ending with a WS row. Do not bind off sts.

NORTH SECONDARY SQUARE

Cont with the first square, join B and knit across all 12 sts.

Row 1 (RS): With a piece of waste yarn and continuing with B, provisionally CO 13 sts—25 sts on needle.

Row 2 (WS): Knit 12 to center st, p1, k to end of row.

Row 3: With C, k11 to 1 st before center st, VDD, k to end of row.

Row 4: K to center st, p1, k to end of row.

Row 5: K to one st before center st, VDD, k to end of row.

Row 6: K to center st, p1, k to end of row.

Rep the last 2 rows until only 13 sts rem.

With B, work Rows 5–6 once (2 rows, 1 garter ridge).

With D, rep Rows 5–6 until 3 sts rem, work one final VDD, tie off last st.

You now have your initial square, plus a three-color square attached and above it.

SOUTH SECONDARY SQUARE

Rotate work so the initial provisionally cast on sts in A are ready to be worked and the RS is facing. Repeat the instructions for North Center Secondary Square.

EAST AND WEST SECONDARY SQUARES

Pick up 12 sts along "east" side of Central Square and work as for North Center Secondary Square.

Repeat for "west" side of Central Square.

Corner Squares

Slip provisionally CO sts from the left edge of any of the Secondary squares onto needle, then continue along the right edge of the next secondary square to the left and PU 12 sts—25 sts total.

Row 1 (RS): With B, knit.

Row 2 (WS): K 12 to center st, p1, k to end of row.

Row 3: With E, k to 1 st before center st, VDD, k to end of row.

Rep last 2 rows until 3 sts rem, work one final VDD, tie off last st.

Rep Corner Square around rem 3 corners. You now have a square made up of 9 smaller squares.

> **TIP:** When picking up sts, use a circular needle to make arrangement of stitches for working easier.

Log Cabin Layout

In the Log Cabin layout, the pieces are laid out North/West, North/West, then East/South, East/South.

LOG ONE

Working along the North edge of the 9-sq mitered section, PU 36 sts, 12 from each square. Arrange sts so you are ready to work a RS row. Remember to catch the first st of each edge in every row with waste yarn, which will make picking up stitches in subsequent rows much easier (see Tip for Picking Up Stitches).

Rows 1–2: With B, knit all sts.

Rows 3–14: With F, knit all sts. Either slip these to a piece of waste yarn, or use a separate circ needle to hold these sts to use later.

You should have a log of Color F with a base of Color B, with waste yarn on either edge on which are held 7 sts.

LOG TWO

Working along the East edge of the 9-sq mitered section, PU 36 sts as for Log One, plus the 7 at the East end of Log One—43 sts.

Rows 1–2: With B, knit all sts.

Rows 3–14: With C, knit all sts. Slip these to a piece of waste yarn or a separate circ needle.

You should have a log of Color C with a base of Color B, with waste yarn on either edge on which are held 7 sts.

LOG THREE

PU the 7 sts at the North edge of Log Two and the 36 sts left from Log One—43 sts.

Rows 1–2: With B, knit all sts.

Rows 3–14: With A, knit all sts.

You should have a log of Color A with a base of Color B, with waste yarn on either edge on which are held 7 sts.

LOG FOUR

PU the 43 sts along the East edge of Log Two and the 7 sts from the edge of Log Three—50 sts.

Rows 1–2: With B, knit all sts.

Rows 3–14: With E, knit all sts.

You should have a log of Color E with a base of Color B, with waste yarn on either edge on which are held 7 sts.

LOG FIVE

PU 7 sts each from the West edges of Logs Three and One plus 36 along the West edge of the 9-sq mitered section—50 sts.

Rows 1–2: With B, knit all sts.

Rows 3–14: With F, knit all sts.

You should have a log of Color F with a base of Color B, with waste yarn on either edge on which are held 7 sts.

LOG SIX

PU 7 sts each from the South edges of Logs Four and Two plus 36 along the South edge of the 9-sq mitered section plus 7 from the South edge of Log Five—57 sts.

Rows 1–2: With B, knit all sts.

Rows 3–14: With C, knit all sts.

You should have a log of Color C with a base of Color B, with waste yarn on either edge on which are held 7 sts.

LOG SEVEN

PU the 50 sts left from Log Five and the 7 sts at the West edge of Log Six—57 sts.

Rows 1–2: With B, knit all sts.

Rows 3–14: With A, knit all sts.

You should have a log of Color A with a base of Color B, with waste yarn on either edge on which are held 7 sts.

LOG EIGHT

PU the 57 sts from Log Six and the 7 sts from the South end of Log Seven—64 sts.

Rows 1–2: With B, knit all sts.

Rows 3–14: With E, knit all sts.

You should have a log of Color E with a base of Color B, with waste yarn on either edge on which are held 7 sts.

LOG NINE

PU 7 sts each at the North edges of Logs Seven and Five, the 43 sts left from Log Three and 7 sts at the North edge of Log Four—64 sts.

Rows 1–2: With B, knit all sts.

Rows 3–14: With F, knit all sts. Either slip these to a piece of waste yarn, or use a separate circ needle to hold these sts to use later.

You should have a log of Color F with a base of Color B, with waste yarn on either edge on which are held 7 sts.

LOG TEN

PU 7 sts each at the East edges of Logs Eight and Six, the 50 sts left from Log Four, and 7 sts at the East edge of Log Nine—71 sts.

Rows 1–2: With B, knit all sts.

Rows 3–14: With C, knit all sts. Slip these to a piece of waste yarn or a separate circ needle.

You should have a log of Color C with a base of Color B, with waste yarn on either edge on which are held 7 sts.

LOG ELEVEN

PU the 7 sts at the North edge of Log Ten and the 64 sts left from Log Nine—71 sts.

Rows 1 –2: With B, knit all sts.

Rows 3–14: With A, knit all sts.

You should have a log of Color A with a base of Color B, with waste yarn on either edge on which are held 7 sts.

LOG TWELVE

PU the 71 sts along the East edge of Log Ten and the 7 sts from the edge of Log Eleven—78 sts.

Rows 1–2: With B, knit all sts.

Rows 3–14: With E, knit all sts.

You should have a log of Color E with a base of Color B, with waste yarn on either edge on which are held 7 sts.

LOG THIRTEEN

PU 7 sts each from the West edges of Logs Eleven and Nine plus 57 sts along the West edge of Log Seven plus 7 from the West edge of Log Eight—78 sts.

Rows 1–2: With B, knit all sts.

Rows 3–14: With F, knit all sts.

You should have a log of Color F with a base of Color B, with waste yarn on either edge on which are held 7 sts.

LOG FOURTEEN

PU 7 sts each from the South edges of Logs Twelve and Ten plus 64 along the South edge of Log Eight plus 7 from the South edge of Log Thirteen—85 sts.

Rows 1–2: With B, knit all sts.

Rows 3–14: With C, knit all sts.

You should have a log of Color C with a base of Color B, with waste yarn on either edge on which are held 7 sts.

LOG FIFTEEN

PU 7 sts from the West edge of Log Fourteen and the 78 sts at the West edge of Log Thirteen—85 sts.

Rows 1–2: With B, knit all sts.

Rows 3–14: With A, knit all sts.

You should have a log of Color A with a base of Color B, with waste yarn on either edge on which are held 7 sts.

LOG SIXTEEN

PU the 85 sts from Log Fourteen and the 7 sts from the South end of Log Fifteen—92 sts.

Rows 1–2: With B, knit all sts.

Rows 3–14: With E, knit all sts.

You should have a log of Color E with a base of Color B, with waste yarn on either edge on which are held 7 sts.

Border

Rnd 1: With B and working around the entire circumference of the piece, PU&K 361.

Rnd 2 and all even rnds: Purl all sts in the same color used in the prev round.

Rnd 3: With D, [knit to 3 sts before next corner, kfb, place marker (pm), k4, pm, kfb] four times—8 markers around the work, inc of 8 sts, 369 total sts.

Rnd 5: With C, [knit to 1 st before next marker, kfb, sm, k4, sm, kfb] four times—377 sts.

Rnds 7–10: Rep Rnds 5–6—393 sts.

Rnds 11–12: With D, rep Rnds 5–6—401 sts.

Rnds 13–16: With F, rep Rnds 5–6—417 sts.

Rnds 17–18: Rep Rnds 11–12—425 sts.

Rnds 19–24: With A, rep Rnds 5–6—449 sts.

Rnds 25–26: Rep Rnds 11–12—457 sts.

Rnd 27 and all rem rnds: With E, rep Rnds 5–6 until there are 537 sts. Bind off all sts loosely.

Finishing

Weave in ends. Steam block piece. Fold square garment along white dotted line on Log Cabin Layout diagram.

Stitch edges together where black dashed lines would meet (creating armholes at either end of the white dashed line).

If desired, with a strand of E and a size G-6 (4 mm) crochet hook, make a 15 st chain at the point where two corners are sewn together, and sew a shank button at the opposite point where two corners are sewn together. Use this as a closure for the garment, which can be worn with either edge as the top/bottom edge.

Lace Cuff Shrug

A very simple sweater, the yarn does all the work in this piece! A bit of increasing and decreasing, a tiny bit of lace and a short sleeve seam will create a shrug you can wear year round.

To make this into an even easier project, don't work the cuffs as lace. Simply work them in garter stitch, increasing needle size every eight rows to create a ruffled effect.

Sizes

To fit bust size 32 (42, 52)"/81.5 (107, 132.5) cm

Finished Measurements

Body width: 24 (30, 36)"/61 (76.5, 92) cm
Body length: 40 (50, 60)"/102 (127.5, 153) cm

Skill Level

Easy

Yarn

Berroco Elements, medium weight #4 yarn (51% wool, 49% nylon; 153 yd./140 m per 1.75 oz./50 g ball)
• 3 (5, 7) skeins #4970 Iodine (Yarn A)
Berroco Ultra Alpaca Fine, super fine weight #1 yarn (50% wool, 30% nylon, 20% alpaca; 144 yd./131 m per 1.75 oz./50 g skein)
• 1 (2, 2) skeins #1201 Winter White (Yarn B)

Needles and Other Materials

• US 8 (5 mm) needles
• US 6 (4 mm) circular needle
• Waste yarn
• 8 (9, 10) stitch markers
• Yarn needle

Gauge

20 sts x 28 rows in St st in Yarn A on size US 8 (5 mm) needles = 4"/10 cm square
Adjust needle size if necessary to obtain gauge.

Stitches & Techniques

PU&K (pick up & knit)

Insert needle into next stitch, stabbing all the way from the right side to the wrong side of the work. Wrap a loop around the needle, pull the loop through, creating a knit stitch.

VDD (vertical double decrease)

Sl 2 sts as if to work k2tog-R, k1, pass slipped sts over—decrease of 2 sts.

VDI (vertical double increase)

K into front of st, yo, k into back of same stitch.

Left Sleeve

With A and a piece of waste yarn, provisionally cast on 44 (56, 64) sts (see page 118 for how to work a provisional cast-on).

Working in St st (K on RS, P on WS) inc 1 st at each edge every other row 38 (48, 58) times—120 (152, 180) sts. Work even with no further inc for approx 8 (8, 12) rows more, until piece meas 12 (15, 18)"/30.5 (38.5, 46) cm from cast on. Mark this row with a piece of waste yarn.

Body

Cont in St st, working even with no further inc or dec until piece meas 16 (20, 24)"/41 (51, 61) cm from row marked with waste yarn. Mark this current row with a second piece of waste yarn.

Right Sleeve

Cont in St st for approx 8 (8, 12) rows, then begin decreasing 1 st at each edge every other row 38 (48, 58) times—44 (56, 64) sts rem.
If necessary, work even until second sleeve meas same as first sleeve, ending with a WS row. *Do not bind off sts.*

UNDERARM SEAMS

Fold piece in half lengthwise from cuff to cuff and sew the underarm seam beg at one cuff and working to the row marked with waste yarn. Repeat for opposite seam.

CUFF

With Yarn B and smaller needles, PU&K 56 (63, 70) sts around lower sleeve edge. Place marker to note start of round.
Rep Lace Cuff patt following chart or text below in Rnds 1–31 8 (9, 10) times around work, placing a marker between each rep if desired.
Work Rnds 32–33 four times (8 rounds total).
Work Rnds 34–35 twice (4 rounds total).
BO all sts loosely.

Lace Cuff Pattern

Rep all rnds 8 (9, 10) times around work.
Rnd 1: [K3, yo, k4].
Rnds 2–4: Knit all sts.
Rnd 5: [K3, yo, k1, yo, k4].
Rnds 6–8: [K3, p3, k4].
Rnd 9: [K3, yo, p3, yo, k4].
Rnd 10: [K3, p5, k4].
Rnd 11: [K3, yo, p1, VDD, p1, yo, k4].
Rnd 12: [K3, p2, k1, p2, k4].
Rnd 13: [K3, yo, p2, sl 1, p2, yo, k4].
Rnd 14: [K3, p3, k1, p3, k4].
Rnd 15: [K3, yo, p2, VDD, p2, yo, k4].
Rnd 16: Rep Row 14.
Rnd 17: [K3, p3, sl 1, p3, k3, yo, k1, yo].
Rnd 18: [K3, p3, k1, p3, k3, p1, k1, p1].
Rnd 19: [K3, p3, sl 1, p3, k3, yo, p1, sl 1, p1, yo].
Rnd 20: [K3, p3, k1, p3, k3, p2, k1, p2].
Rnd 21: [K3, p3, sl 1, p3, k3, yo, p2, sl 1, p2, yo].
Rnd 22: [K3, p3, k1, p3] twice.
Rnd 23: [K3, p3, sl 1, p3] twice.
Rnds 24, 26, 28, and 30: Rep Row 22.
Rnds 25, 27, and 29: Rep Row 23.
Rnd 31: [K3, p3, VDI, p3] twice.
Rnds 32–33: [K3, p3] rep around work.
Rnd 34: Knit all sts
Rnd 35: Purl all sts.

Finishing

Weave in ends. Steam block piece, taking special care to open up lace in cuffs fully.

Finished Measurements

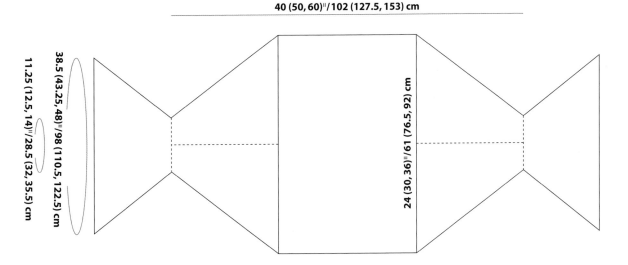

40 (50, 60)"/102 (127.5, 153) cm

11.25 (12.5, 14)"/28.5 (32, 35.5) cm

38.5 (43.25, 48)"/98 (110.5, 122.5) cm

24 (30, 36)"/61 (76.5, 92) cm

16 (20, 24)"/41 (51, 61) cm   12 (15, 18)"/30.5 (38.5, 46) cm   6.25 (6.25, 6.25)"/16 (16, 16) cm

Lace Cuff Chart

St st
Rev St St
Yo
VDD
Sl st (wyws)
VDI

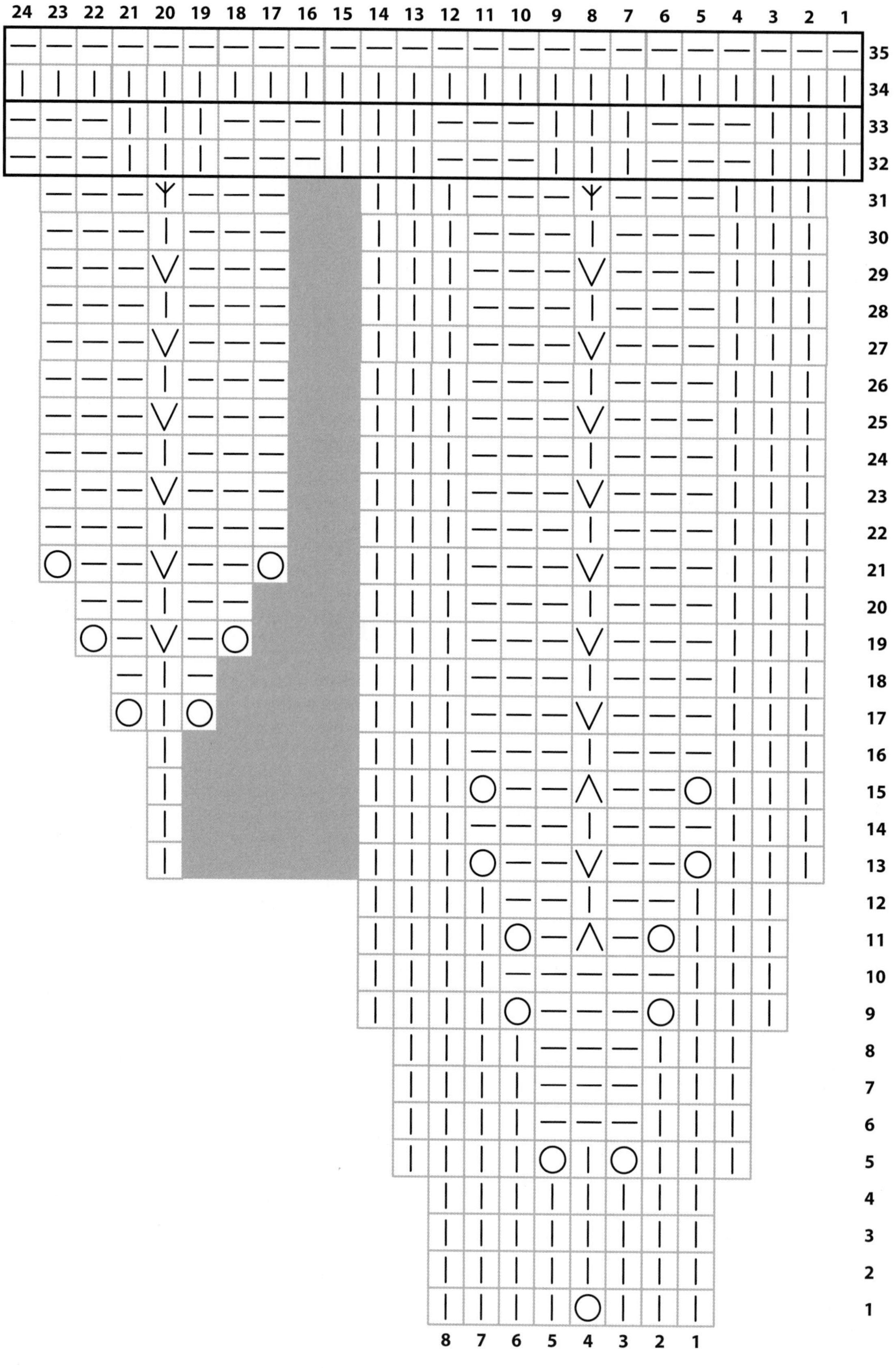
24 23 22 21 20 19 18 17 16 15 14 13 12 11 10 9 8 7 6 5 4 3 2 1
35
34
33
32
31
30
29
28
27
26
25
24
23
22
21
20
19
18
17
16
15
14
13
12
11
10
9
8
7
6
5
4
3
2
1
8 7 6 5 4 3 2 1

Lace Knit Shrug

F lattering, sensible, and the perfect dress-up piece for a strapless gown or simple tank top. This small, useful piece will see you through many a chilly evening or over-air conditioned dinner!

Sizes

To fit bust 32 (38, 44, 50)"/81.5 (97, 112, 127.5) cm

Finished Measurements

Sleeve length: 20 (21, 22, 23)"/51 (53.5, 56, 58.5) cm
Back depth: 8 (8^1/$_2$, 9, 9^1/$_2$)"/20.5 (21.5, 23, 24) cm

Skill Level

Intermediate

Yarn

Juno Fiber Arts Alice DK, light weight #3 yarn (70% baby alpaca, 20% silk, 10% cashmere; 247 yd./225 m per 3.5 oz./100 g skein)
- 2 (3, 3, 4) skeins Black Lilac

Needles and Other Materials

- US 7 (4.5 mm) circular needle
- US 6 (4 mm) circular needle
- One 1"/1.25 cm button

Gauge

16.5 sts x 28 rows in lace pattern on US 7 (4.5 mm) needle = 4"/10 cm square
Adjust needle size if necessary to obtain gauge.

Stitch Guide

Dkss Edge (double knit slipped st edge, worked over 5 sts)

This edging is created by slipping and knitting stitches, keeping in mind that whenever stitches are slipped at either edge, the yarn is held *toward* the knitter, regardless of whether the right or wrong side is facing the knitter.
RS Row: {K1, wyrs sl 1, k1, p2}, work in patt to last 5 sts, {p2, k1, wyrs sl 1, k1}.
WS Row: {Wyws sl 1, k1, wyws sl 1, k2}, work in patt to last 5 sts, {k2, wyws sl 1, k1, wyws sl 1}.

K2tog-L (knit 2 tog with a left slant)
Knit 2 stitches together so the working needle is pointing to the left as it enters the stitch (dec will slant to the left); common left-slanting decreases are ssk, k2tog-tbl, or skp.

K2tog-R (knit 2 tog with a right slant)
Knit 2 stitches together so the working needle is pointing to the right as it enters the stitch (dec will slant to the right); most common is k2tog.

Kfb (knit into front and back of one stitch)
Knit into the front and back of the same stitch—increase of 1 st.

Pfb (purl into front and back of one stitch)
Purl into the front and back of the same stitch—increase of 1 st.

VDD (vertical double decrease)
Sl 2 sts as if to work k2tog-R, k1, pass slipped sts over—decrease of 2 sts.

Wyrs sl 1 (with yarn right side, slip 1)
Move yarn to RS of work. Insert RH needle purlwise into st and slip off of LH needle.

Wyws sl 1 (with yarn wrong side, slip 1)
Move yarn to WS of work. Insert RH needle purlwise into st and slip off of LH needle.

Sleeve (Make 2)

With smaller circular needles CO 36 (40, 44, 48) sts, join in round, and place marker to note start of round.
Rnd 1: [K2, p2] rep to end of round.
Cont in k2, p2 ribbing until cuff meas 4 (4^1/$_4$, 3^1/$_2$, 3^1/$_2$)"/10 (11, 9, 9) cm from CO edge.

Lace Shrug

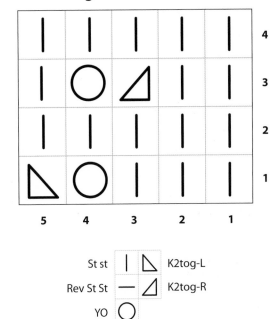

					4
St st		K2tog-L
Rev St St	—	K2tog-R
YO	○	

CUFF INCREASE

Next rnd: Change to larger needles. [K2, pfb, p1] 9 (10, 11, 12) times around work—45 (50, 55, 60) sts.

ESTABLISH LACE PATTERN—LACE SHRUG CHART

Rnd 1: [K3, yo, k2tog-L] rep around work.
Rnds 2 and 4: Knit.
Rnd 3: [K2, k2tog-R, yo, k1] rep around work.
Rep these 4 rnds twice.

SLEEVE INCREASE

Working in patt as est, beg inc as foll:
Next rnd: Kfb, work in patt as est to last st in round, kfb, slip marker.
Next 7 (3, 3, 3) rnds: Work in patt as est with no inc.
Cont in this manner, inc 1 st either side of marker every 8 (4, 4, 4) rnds, incorporating new sts into lace patt. Inc 10 (15, 15, 15) times—65 (80, 85, 90) sts total.
Work even until sleeve meas 20 (21, 22, 23)"/51 (53.5, 56, 58.5) cm from cuff, or desired length. End with Rnd 4 of Lace patt.

Back

Slip both sleeves onto larger needle.

ESTABLISH DKSS EDGE AT FRONT

Note: The dkss edge in this pattern is worked over 5 stitches.
Next row (RS): {K1, wyrs sl 1, k1, p2}, work in patt as est to end of first sleeve. Using any CO method, CO 65 (70, 75, 80) sts between sleeves. Work across second sleeve in patt as est to last 5 sts, {p2, k1, wyrs sl 1, k1}—195 (230, 245, 260) sts.
Next row (WS): {Wyws sl 1, k1, wyws sl 1, k2}, purl 60 (75, 80, 85) sts, k 65 (70, 75, 80) Back sts, p 60 (75, 80, 85) sts to last 5 sts in row, {k2, wyws sl 1, k1, wyws sl 1}.

BEGIN BACK DECREASE

Row 1 (RS): {K1, wyrs sl 1, k1, p2}, work in patt as est for 64 (79, 84, 89) sts, VDD, place marker (pm), k63 (68, 73, 78) sts, pm, VDD, work in patt as est to last 5 sts, {p2, k1, wyrs sl 1, k1}.
Row 2 (WS): {Wyws sl 1, k1, wyws sl 1, k2} purl to marker, knit to next marker, purl to last 5 sts, {k1, wyws sl 1, k1, wyws sl 1}.

continued

Rep last two rows until 114 (138, 140, 152) sts rem. End with a WS row.

NECK EDGE

Next row (RS): Switch to smaller needles and dec across Fronts *only* as foll: {K1, wyrs sl 1, k1, p2}, [k1, k2tog-L] 15 (19, 20, 22) times, k to last 5 sts, {K1, wyrs sl 1, k1, p2}.

Next row (WS): {Wyws sl 1, k1, wyws sl 1, k2}, [p1, p2tog] 15 (19, 20, 22) times, p to last 5 sts, {Wyws sl 1, k1, wyws sl 1, k2}—84 (100, 100, 108) sts.

With no further dec, work 4 rows of St st (K on RS, P on WS), continuing to work either end in dkss edge, and ending with a WS row.

BIND-OFF

Slip the first 2 sts off the LH needle, then slip them back on in reverse order so that what was the first st is now second, and the second st is now first.

[K3, slip 3 sts back to LH needle] five times, creating an extended piece of I-cord to use as a button loop later.

Continuing along neck edge (all sts should be together on LH needle at this point) BO as foll:

1. [K2, k2tog-L, slip 3 sts back onto LH needle] rep until 4 sts rem to be bound off, 7 sts on LH total.
2. K2, VDD, slip 3 sts from RH needle back onto LH needle.
3. K1, VDD, slip 2 sts from RH needle back onto LH needle.
4. VDD. Tie off last st.

Finishing

Steam block piece. Weave in ends. Sew a 1"/1.25 cm button to the left neck edge corresponding to the button loop on the right neck edge.

Row 3 (RS): {Dkss RS edge} work in patt as est to 1 st before marker, sl 1, slip marker (sm), k to next marker, sm, sl 1, work in patt as est to last 5 sts, {dkss RS edge}.

Row 4 (WS): {Dkss WS edge} purl to marker, knit to next marker, purl to last 5 sts, {dkss WS edge}.

Rep last 2 rows 3 (3, 5, 4) times more. Remove markers in last row, then beg dec in each RS row as foll:

Next row (RS): {Dkss RS edge}, work in patt as est to 2 sts before slipped st, VDD, k to next slipped st, VDD, work in patt as est to last 5 sts, {dkss RS edge}.

Next row (WS): {Dkss WS edge}, p across all sts to last 5 sts in row, {dkss WS edge}.

Finished Measurements

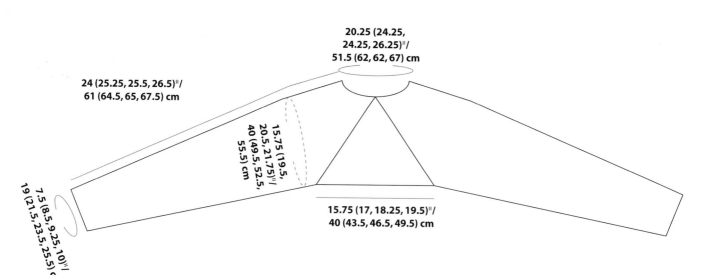

20.25 (24.25, 24.25, 26.25)"/
51.5 (62, 62, 67) cm

24 (25.25, 25.5, 26.5)"/
61 (64.5, 65, 67.5) cm

15.75 (19.5, 20.5, 21.75)"/
40 (49.5, 52.5, 55.5) cm

7.5 (8.5, 9.25, 10)"/
19 (21.5, 23.5, 25.5) cm

15.75 (17, 18.25, 19.5)"/
40 (43.5, 46.5, 49.5) cm

Mitered Ruana

Bold, striking colors in a chunky yarn married with a simple mitering technique make this garment a blast to work up! The ease and drama of wearing such a show-stopping jacket will turn up the volume on every entrance you make.

Sizes

To fit bust 32 (38, 44)"/81.5 (97, 112) cm

Finished Measurements

Width of garment: 48^1/$_2$ (58, 67^1/$_2$)"/123.5 (148, 172) cm
Length of garment: 24^1/$_4$ (29, 33^3/$_4$)"/62 (74, 86) cm

Skill Level

Easy

Yarn

Dragonfly Fibers Super Traveller, bulky weight #5 yarn
(100% superwash merino wool; 107 yd./98 m per ball)
- 3 (4, 6) balls Black Pearl (Color A)
- 3 (4, 6) balls Reluctant Dragon (Color B)
- 4 (6, 8) balls Riptide (Color C)

Needles and Other Materials

- US 10 (6 mm) needles
- Waste yarn

Gauge

10 sts x 21 rows in St st = 4"/10 cm square
Adjust needle size if necessary to obtain gauge.

Notes

- In this pattern odd rows (1, 3, 5) are WS rows. Each segment of the Mitered Ruana starts with a WS row.
- The ruana is designed so that when worn the VDD decrease line should sit directly at the top of the shoulder and run straight down the arm.

Stitch Guide

VDD (vertical double decrease)
Sl 2 sts as if to work k2tog-R, k1, pass slipped sts over—
decrease of 2 sts.

W&T (wrap & turn)
Work the desired number of sts for the short row. Move yarn to RS. Slip next st to the right-hand needle. Move yarn to WS. Return stitch to left-hand needle. Turn and begin working back in the opposite direction.

Body

The body is made up of two sides, Side One and Side Two.

SIDE ONE

With A and a piece of waste yarn, provisionally CO 121 (145, 169) sts. (See page 118 for instructions on how to work a provisional cast-on.)

Row 1 (WS): Knit 60 (72, 84) sts to center st, purl center st, knit to end of row.

Row 2 (RS): K3, k56 (68, 80) sts, VDD, k56 (68, 80) sts, k3—119 (143, 167) sts rem.

Row 3 (WS): K3, purl to last 3 sts, k3.

Row 4 (RS): K to 1 st before VDD from prev RS row, VDD, k to end of row.

Rows 5–8: Rep last 4 rows twice more—113 (137, 161) sts.

Row 9 (WS): With B, knit to center st, purl center st, knit to end of row.

Row 10 (RS): K to 1 st before VDD from prev RS row, VDD, k to end of row—111 (135, 159) sts.

Row 11 (WS): K3, purl to last 3 sts, k3.

Row 12: Rep Row 10.

Row 13 (WS): With C, knit to center st, purl center st, knit to end of row.

Row 14 (RS): K to 1 st before VDD from prev RS row, VDD, k to end of row—107 (131, 155) sts.

Row 15 (WS): K3, purl to last 3 sts, k3.

Row 16: Rep Row 14.

Rows 17–24: Rep Rows 9–16 in the colors specified, working a VDD in the center of every RS row—97 (121, 145) sts.

Rows 25–32: Rep Rows 1–8 in A, working a VDD in the center of every RS row—89 (113, 137) sts.

Cont in patt as est, working Rows 1–32 in the colors specified and working a VDD in the center of every RS row until 57 (69, 81) sts rem—64 (76, 88) rows total.

With A, knit 2 rows, then BO all sts loosely.

Lay the piece you've just knitted flat. Align it so the provisionally cast on sts are at right angles at the top and left edge of the piece. Put a safety pin anywhere along the left provisionally cast-on edge.

SIDE TWO

With A and a piece of waste yarn, provisionally CO 60 (72, 84) sts. Carefully slip the 61 (73, 85) sts along the safety pin side of Side One onto the needle, begining with the center (corner) st and working to the end of the row—121 (145, 169) sts total on needle.

Refer to diagram for visual assistance.

Work 64 (76, 88) rows as for Side One.

With A, knit 2 rows, then BO all sts loosely.

Mitered Ruana Chart

Note: Chart shows only main st part of each row. See text for full instructions.

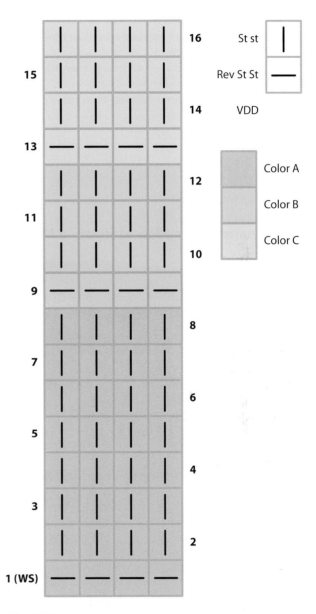

St st

Rev St St

VDD

Color A

Color B

Color C

Collar

Carefully slip the 60 (72, 84) sts remaining provisionally cast-on sts from each top edge of each side onto one needle—120 (144, 168) sts.

Row 1: With B k3, [p2, k2] rep to last 5 sts, end p2, k3.

Cont working in rib with garter edges as est for 4 rows.

Next row: With C work in rib as est to last 5 sts, W&T.

Next row: Work in rib as est to last 5 sts on opposite end of row, W&T (5 sts unworked on either end of row).

continued

Next row: Work in rib as est to 4 sts before last W&T (9 sts unworked at end of row).

Rep last row 11 times (a total of 12 repeats)—there should be 29 sts unworked at either end of the row.

Next row: Work in rib as est, slipping wraps from sts in prev rows up onto needle and working along with wrapped st.

Next row: Rep last row, all wrapped sts should now be dealt with.

With B, work 4 rows in rib as est with no further short-row shaping.

With A, work 2 rows in garter (knitting all sts). Bind off all sts loosely.

Finishing

Weave in ends. Steam block piece.

Mitered Ruana Schematic and Finished Measurements

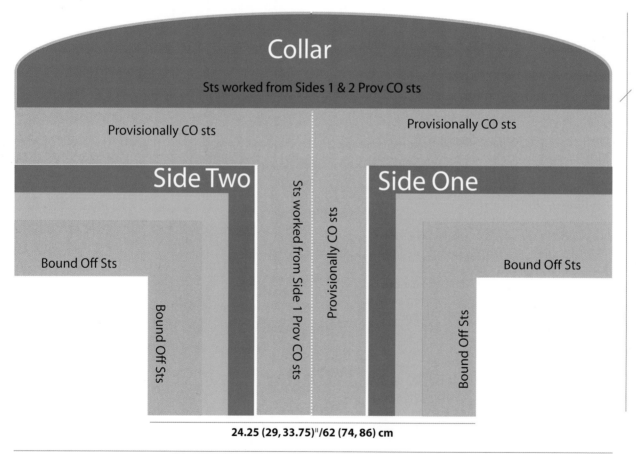

24.25 (29, 33.75)"/62 (74, 86) cm

48.5 (58, 67.5)"/123.5 (148, 172) cm

Morse
Cowl

The stitch pattern in this simple cowl is ridiculously easy, giving the appearance of dots and dashes circling around the piece, thus the name Morse Cowl. When slipping stitches in this pattern, it's good to remember that the default is to slip a stitch purlwise with the yarn to the wrong side, unless otherwise directed by a pattern.

Sizes

One Size

Finished Measurements

Circumference: 26"/66 cm
Length: 13"/33 cm

Skill Level

Easy

Yarn

Lorna's Laces Shepherd Worsted, medium weight #4 yarn (100% superwash wool; 225 yd./205 m per 4 oz./114 g ball)
• 2 balls Kerfuffle (MC)
Lorna's Laces Pearl, medium weight #4 yarn (51% silk, 49% bamboo; 220 yd./201 m per 3.5 oz./100g ball)
• 2 balls Motherlode (CC)

Needles and Other Materials

• US 7 (4.5 mm) circular needle
• Stitch marker

Gauge

16 sts x 40 rows in Sl St patt = 4"/10 cm square
Adjust needle size if necessary to obtain gauge.

Stitch Guide

Wyrs sl 1 (with yarn right side, slip 1)
Move yarn to RS of work. Insert RH needle purlwise into st and slip onto RH needle.

Wyws sl 1 (with yarn wrong side, slip 1)
Move yarn to WS of work. Insert RH needle purlwise into st and slip onto RH needle.

Morse Cowl

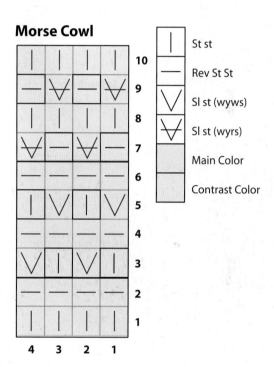

	St st
—	Rev St St
V	Sl st (wyws)
⅄	Sl st (wyrs)
	Main Color
	Contrast Color

Cowl

With MC, CO 104, join in round, and place marker to note start of round.
Work Rnds 1–2 of Morse Cowl Chart twice, creating 4 rounds of garter st (knit 1 round, purl 1 round).

BEGIN SLIP STITCH PATTERN

Work Rnds 3–6 of Morse Cowl Chart around all sts as foll:
Rnd 3: [With CC k1, wyws sl 1] rep around work.
Rnd 4: With MC, purl all sts.
Rnd 5: [With CC wyws sl 1, k1] rep around work.
Rnd 6: Rep Rnd 2.
Rep Rnds 3–6 nine times more (40 rows total in slip st patt).

GARTER BAND

With MC, work 2 rounds in garter (Rnds 1–2 of chart).

REVERSE SLIP STITCH PATTERN

Work Rnds 7–10 of Morse Cowl Chart around all sts as foll:

Rnd 7: [With CC p1, wyrs sl 1] rep around work.

Rnd 8: With MC, knit all sts.

Rnd 9: [With CC wyrs sl 1, p1] rep around work.

Rnd 10: Rep Rnd 8.

Rep Rnds 7–10 nine times more (40 rnds total in Rev slip st patt).

GARTER BAND

With MC, work 2 rounds in garter (Rnds 1–2 of chart).

SLIP STITCH PATTERN

Work Rnds 3–6 of Morse Cowl Chart around all sts as foll:

Rnd 3: [With CC k1, wyws sl 1] rep around work.

Rnd 4: With MC, purl all sts.

Rnd 5: [With CC wyws sl 1, k 1] rep around work.

Rnd 6: Rep Rnd 2.

Rep Rnds 3–6 nine times more (40 rnds total in slip st patt).

GARTER BAND

With MC, work 4 rounds in garter (Rnds 1–2 of chart twice). With MC, bind off all sts loosely.

Finishing

Weave in ends. Steam block.

Finished Measurements

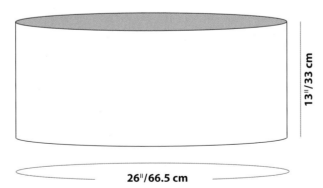

13"/33 cm

26"/66.5 cm

Plaid Vest

here are several ways to work plaid in knitting, but this is my favorite technique! I stumbled onto this when trying to figure a way to work corrugated rib more easily, and have used it for many garments and accessories. It's a brilliant way to use up a small amount of stash yarn or blend seemingly non-friendly colors into a beautiful palette.

Sizes

To fit bust 32 (38, 44, 50, 56)"/81.5 (97, 112, 127.5, 143) cm

Finished Measurements

Bust: 38 (44, 50, 56, 62)"/97 (112, 127.5, 143, 158) cm
Total length: $19^{1}/_{4}$ ($20^{1}/_{4}$, $21^{1}/_{4}$, $22^{1}/_{4}$, $23^{1}/_{4}$)"/49 (51.5, 54, 57, 59.5) cm

Skill Level

Intermediate

Yarn

Leilani Arts Soft Donegal, worsted weight #4 yarn (100% merino wool; 210 yd./190 m per 3.5 oz./100 g ball)
- 3 (4, 5, 6, 8) balls Marine Blue (Color A)
- 1 (1, 2, 2, 3) balls Charcoal (Color B)
- 1 (1, 2, 2, 3) balls Medium Gray (Color C)
- 1 (1, 2, 2, 3) balls Olive (Color D)
- 1 (1, 2, 2, 3) balls Bainin (Color E)
- 1 (1, 2, 2, 3) balls Deep Red (Color F)

Needles and Other Materials

- US 7 (4.5 mm) circular needle
- US 8 (5 mm) circular needle
- Yarn needle

Gauge

16 sts x 32 rows in Plaid patt = 4"/10 cm square
Adjust needle size if necessary to obtain gauge.

Notes

- It's not necessary to mirror, or reverse, the plaid motif across the front. Begin and end the Plaid patt at the same point on the chart for both Left and Right Fronts.

Stitch Guide

PU (pick up)

Using the knitting needle only, with no source of yarn, pick up a loop from the existing fabric to create a stitch on the needle.

PU&K (pick up & knit)

Insert needle into next stitch, stabbing all the way from the right side to the wrong side of the work. Wrap a loop around the needle, pull the loop through, creating a knit stitch.

W&T (wrap & turn)

Work the desired number of sts for the short row. Move yarn to RS. Slip next st to the right-hand needle. Move yarn to WS. Return stitch to left-hand needle. Turn and begin working back in the opposite direction.

Wyws sl 1 (with yarn wrong side, slip 1)

Move yarn to WS of work. Insert RH needle purlwise into st and slip onto RH needle.

Stitch Pattern

Plaid

Row 1 (RS): [With E, k3; with B, k7; with E, k3; with C, k5] rep across work.
Slip work back so a second RS row is ready to be worked.
Row 2 (RS): With Slip St Color [k1, wyws sl 1] rep across work.
Turn work.
Row 3 (WS): Purl all sts, keeping to the vertical stripes of color as est in Row 1 and working *only* with those colors.
Slip work back so a second WS row is ready to be worked.
Row 4 (WS): With Slip St Color [wyws sl 1, p1] rep across work.

Back

With A and smaller needles, CO 76 (88, 100, 112, 124) sts.
Work in k2, p2 ribbing for 4 rows.
Change to larger needles and begin working in St st (knit on RS, purl on WS).
Work even with no shaping until work meas 19 (20, 21, 22, 23)"/48.5 (51, 53.5, 56, 58.5) cm from ribbing. Slip all sts to waste yarn to work later.

Plaid Chart

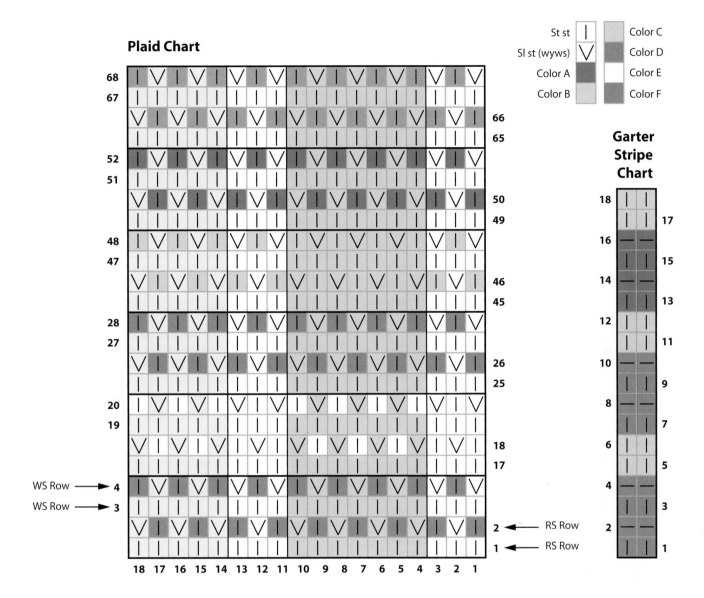

continued

TIP: Though you could work the Left and Right Fronts at the same time, because of the many strands of yarn required for working the plaid motif, it will be easier to work each Front separately.

Left Front

With A and smaller needles, CO 50 (56, 62, 68, 74) sts.
Work in k2, p2 ribbing for 4 rows.
Change to larger (circular) needles and establish plaid patt as foll:

Row 1 (RS): Beg with St 1, Row 1, work across all sts of Plaid Chart 2 (2, 2, 3, 3) times, then work to st 8 (14, 20, 5, 11) of chart. Slide work back on needle so a second RS row is ready to be worked.

Row 2 (RS): With Color D [k1, sl 1] rep across work. Turn work.

Row 3 (WS): Purl all sts, keeping to the vertical stripes of color as est in Row 1 and working *only* with those colors. Slide work back along needle so a secnd WS row is ready to be worked.

Row 4 (WS): With Color D [p1, sl 1] rep across work. Turn work.

Rows 5–16: Rep Rows 1–4 three times.

Rows 17–24: Rep Rows 1–4, substituting Color E for Color D in Rows 2 and 4.

Rows 25–44: Rep Rows 1–4, sub Color F for Color D.

Rows 45–48: Rep Rows 1–4, sub Color C for Color D.

Rows 49–64: Rep Rows 1–4, sub Color A for Color D.

Rows 65–72: Rep Rows 1–4, sub Color B for Color D.

Cont in this manner, working vertical stripes as est and alternating the slip stitch colors in Rows 2 and 4 as written above (and shown in chart), until piece meas 6^1/$_2$ (7, 7^1/$_2$, 8, 8^1/$_2$)"/16.5 (18, 19, 20.5, 21.5) cm from ribbing.

> **TIP:** Set up each vertical stripe with its own source of yarn. For a narrow (3-st) stripe, a long strand will work fine. For a wider stripe, a small ball would be useful.

Neck Shaping

Cont in Plaid Patt as est, BO 1 st at neck edge every 6 rows 14 (14, 15, 15, 16) times *and at the same time*, when work measures 5^1/$_4$ (5^1/$_2$, 5^1/$_2$, 5^3/$_4$, 5^3/$_4$)"/13.5 (14, 14, 14.5, 14.5) cm from start of neck BO, change to Garter Stripe Patt as follows while continuing to BO at neck edge.

GARTER STRIPE PATTERN

Rows 1–4: With D, knit (garter st).
Row 5: With B, knit.
Row 6: Purl.
Rows 7–10: With F, knit.
Rows 11–12: Rep Rows 5–6.
Rows 13–16: With A, knit.
Rows 17–18: Rep Rows 5–6.
Rep these 16 rows while continuing to BO at neck edge, until 24 (29, 34, 39, 44) sts rem for shoulder. Work even with no further decreasing until Left Front meas same as back in total length. Slip rem shoulder sts to waste yarn to work later.

Right Front

Work as for Left Front, binding off neck sts at the opposite edge of the work. Slip rem shoulder sts to waste yarn to work later.

JOINING FRONTS AND BACK

Slip back sts onto one needle, slip both fronts onto a second needle, arranged so the neck openings are at the center. Align the pieces so the right sides are facing each other and join the 24 (29, 34, 39, 44) sts at each shoulder in a 3-needle bind-off (see page 119 for photo-illustrated instructions) as follows in Color A. Keep 28 (30, 32, 34, 36) center back sts on circ needle.
1. Place the two pieces on knitting needles so the right sides of each piece are facing each other with the needles parallel.
2. Insert a third needle one size larger through the leading edge of the first stitch on each needle (knitwise).

3. Knit these stitches together as one, leaving 1 st on RH needle.
4. Repeat steps 2–3 and slip older stitch on LH needle over newer stitch.
Repeat step 4 until all sts are bound off. Cut yarn, pull through last stitch.

Collar

Using either end of circ needle on which center Back sts are resting to PU 42 (44, 45, 47, 48) sts down each front edge to the cast on edge—112 (118, 122, 128, 132) total Collar sts.
Row 1: [K2, p2] rep across all sts, end k2.
Row 2 and all subsequent rows: Work in k2, p2 rib as est. Work a total of 6 rows in rib.

SHORT-ROW SECTION

Next row: Work 88 (94, 98, 104, 108) sts in rib as est, W&T (24 sts rem unworked between W&T and end of row).
Next row: Work 64 (70, 74, 80, 84) sts in rib as est, W&T (24 sts rem unworked between W&T and end of row).
Next row: Work to 4 sts before last W&T, W&T.
Rep last row 8 (8, 10, 12, 12) times times—32 (38, 34, 32, 36) sts rem between last W&Ts.
Next two rows: Work in k2, p2 rib as est across all sts, slipping wraps from W&Ts up onto needle and working them along with slipped st.
Cont in k2, p2 rib for another 6 rows. Bind off all sts loosely in rib.

Join Body Sides

With a yarn needle and a strand of A, sew together the left and right sides of the body. Begin at the hem and work up until an 8 (8, 9, 10, 10)"/20.5 (20.5, 23, 25.5, 25.5) cm opening is left for the armholes on each side.

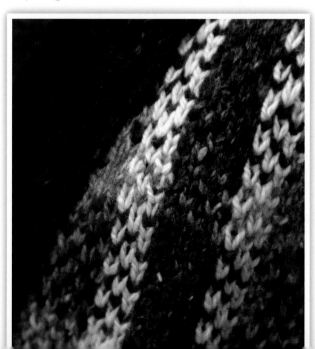

Armhole Cuffs

With a piece of A and circular needles, begining at the bottom edge of the armhole, PU&K 64 (64, 72, 80, 80) sts around armhole. Place marker to note start of round. Work in k2, p2 ribbing for 6 rows. BO all sts loosely.

Finishing

Weave in ends. Steam block piece.

Finished Measurements

19 (22, 25, 28, 31)"/48.5 (56, 64, 71.5, 79) cm

**6 (7.25, 8.5, 9.75, 11)"/
15.5 (18.5, 21.5, 25, 28) cm**

8 (8, 9, 10, 10)"/
20.5 (20.5, 23, 25.5, 25.5) cm

19 (20, 21, 22, 23)"/48.5 (51, 53.5, 56, 58.5) cm

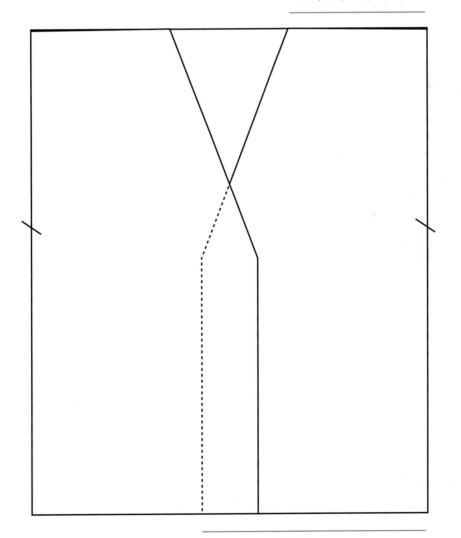

**12.5 (14, 15.5, 17, 18.5)"/
32 (35.5, 39.5, 43.5, 47) cm**

38 (44, 50, 56, 62)"/97 (112, 127.5, 143, 158) cm

Short Kimono Cardigan

A perfect first garment for a new knitter, with very little shaping and simple finishing techniques, this kimono cardigan will be a lovely introduction to the concept of a provisional cast-on, ribbing, and picking up stiches.

Sizes

To fit bust 32 (38, 44, 50)"/81.5 (97, 112, 127.5) cm

Skill Level

Beginner

Yarn

Dream in Color Perfectly Posh Single Ply, super fine weight #1 yarn (70% merino wool, 10% mohair, 10% silk, 10% cashmere; 360 yd./328 m per 3.5 oz./100 g skein)
• 3 (5, 8, 12) skeins Rose Anguish

Needles and Other Materials

• US 8 (5 mm) circular needle
• Waste yarn

Gauge

16 sts x 20 rows in Lace patt = 4"/10 cm square
Adjust needle size if necessary to obtain gauge.

Stitch Guide

PU&K (pick up & knit)

Insert needle into next stitch, stabbing all the way from the right side to the wrong side of the work. Wrap a loop around the needle, pull the loop through, creating a knit stitch.

Body

Cast on 104 (124, 144, 164) sts.

Work in k2, p2 ribbing for 4 rows, as follows:

Row 1 (WS): [K2, p2] rep around.

Row 2: [K2, p2] rep around, working knits into knit sts, and purls into purl sts.

Repeat Row 2 two more times.

Change to St st (knit on RS, purl on WS) and work even until work meas 16^1/$_2$ (19^1/$_2$, 22^1/$_2$, 25^1/$_2$)"/42 (49.5, 57.5, 65) cm from cast on.

Next row (RS): Knit 52 (62, 72, 82) sts, slip these onto a piece of waste yarn to work later, k to the end of the row.

Next row (WS): Purl to first slipped st, provisionally CO 52 (62, 72, 82) sts—104 (124, 144, 164) sts total. (See page 118 for how to work a provisional cast-on.)

Cont in St st for another 15^1/$_2$ (18^1/$_2$, 21^1/$_2$, 24^1/$_2$)"/39.5 (47, 55, 62.5) cm.

Work 4 rows in k2, p2 ribbing. Bind off all sts.

Fold piece lengthwise, with edges touching, so the provisionally cast on sts and the sts on waste yarn run down the center of the piece (see schematic).

Working in from either k2, p2 rib edge, sew edges together 6^3/$_4$ (7^1/$_2$, 8^1/$_2$, 10)"/17 (19, 21.5, 25.5) cm on each side of bottom edge as shown in schematic.

WAISTBAND

Working along the bottom edge of the piece, starting at the center front opening and with the RS facing you, PU&K 34 (38, 42, 50) along the bottom to the seam.

Continue around the back bottom edge, PU&K 62 (74, 90, 102) sts to the seam. PU&K 34 (38, 42, 50) sts along the bottom to the center front opening—130 (150, 174, 202) sts around waistband total.

Next row: K2, [p2, k2] rep around to the end of the row.

Cont in ribbing as est until waistband meas 2^1/$_2$" from picked up sts, or desired length.

COLLAR

With RS of work facing you, PU&K 9 sts along waistband end, slip 52 (62, 72, 82) sts from waste yarn onto needle, then slip the second set of 52 (62, 72, 82) sts waste yarn sts onto the needle. PU&K 9 sts along the opposite waisband end—122 (142, 162, 182) total for collar.

Work in k2, p2 ribbing until collar meas 4"/10 cm or desired length.

Bind off all sts loosely in rib.

Finishing

Weave in all ends. Steam block piece.

Finished Measurements

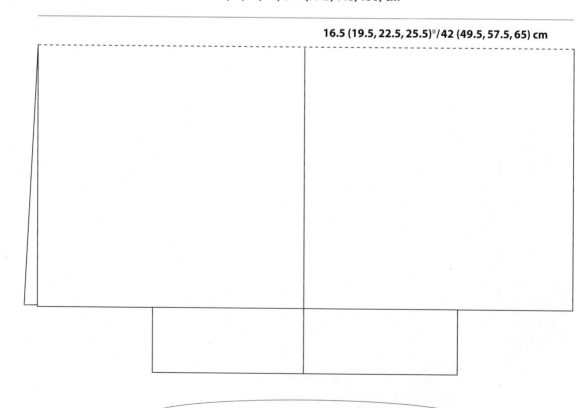

33 (39, 45, 51)"/84 (99.5, 115, 130) cm

16.5 (19.5, 22.5, 25.5)"/42 (49.5, 57.5, 65) cm

26 (31, 36, 41)"/66.5 (79, 92, 104.5) cm

32.5 (38.75, 45, 51.25)"/ 83 (99, 115, 130.5) cm

Stained Glass Armery

The excitement in this long-sleeved top comes from the use of slipped stitches to carry color up from previous rounds. Only one color is ever used in any round, but the effect is as if stranded colorwork had been employed.

Sizes

Small (Medium, Large, Extra-Large)

Finished Measurements

Wrist circumference: 8 (8^1/$_4$, 8^1/$_2$, 8^3/$_4$)"/20.5 (21, 21.5, 22.5) cm

Upper arm circumference: 12 (13, 14^1/$_2$, 15^1/$_2$)"/30.5 (33, 37, 39.5) cm

Sleeve length: 12 (13, 14^1/$_2$, 15^1/$_2$)"/30.5 (33, 37, 39.5) cm

Back depth: 13 (13^3/$_4$, 15^1/$_4$, 16)"/33 (35, 39, 41) cm

Skill Level

Easy

Yarn

Anzula Cricket, light weight #3 yarn (80% superwash merino, 10% cashmere, 10% nylon; 250 yd./228 m per 3.5 oz./100 g skein)

- 1 skein Black (Color A)
- 1 skein Daffodil (Color B)
- 1 skein Grape (Color C)
- 1 skein Olive (Color D)
- 1 skein Madam (Color E)
- 1 skein Blueberry (Color F)

Needles and Other Materials

- US 6 (4 mm) circular needle
- US 5 (3.75 mm) circular needle
- Yarn needle

Gauge

22 sts x 26 rows in St st on US 6 (4 mm) needles = 4"/10 cm square

Adjust needle size if necessary to obtain gauge.

Stitch Guide

PU&K (pick up & knit)

Insert needle into next stitch, stabbing all the way from the right side to the wrong side of the work. Wrap a loop around the needle and pull the loop through, creating a knit stitch.

Stitch Pattern

K2, P2 Rib

Row 1 (WS): [K2, p2] rep across.

Row 2 (RS): [K2, p2] rep across, working knits into knit sts, and purls into purl sts.

Sleeve (Make 2)

CUFF

With A and larger needle, CO 48 (48, 56, 56) sts. Join to work in the round, and place marker to note start of round.

Change to smaller needles and work in K2, P2 Rib for 8 (8^1/$_4$, 8^1/$_2$, 8^3/$_4$)"/20.5 (21, 21.5, 22.5) cm.

Inc 4 (8, 4, 8) sts evenly around last round of ribbing—52 (56, 60, 64) sts.

> **TIP:** It's not necessary to cut or break A. It can be carried up along the WS of the work. Catch the strand of A with the contrasting color every two or three rounds to prevent very long floats up the wrong side of the work.

BEGIN COLORWORK

Following Stained Glass Armery Chart work next 8 rnds as foll:

Rnd 1: With B, [k1, sl 1, k2] rep around work.

Rnd 2: [K1, p1, k2] rep around work.

Rnds 3–6: Knit all sts.

Rnd 7: With A, [k1, sl 1, k2] rep around work.

Rnd 8: [K1, p1, k2] rep around work.

Rep the above 8 rows, swapping Color C for B, then D for C, E for D, etc., until each of the non-A colors has been used (40 rows total for all colors), *and at the same time, begin Sleeve Shaping as follows.*

SLEEVE SHAPING

Inc 1 st on either side of stitch marker every 4th round, incorporating the new stitches into the colorwork patt, until stitch count reaches 72 (76, 84, 88) sts.

Work even, cont in colorwork patt, until sleeve meas 12 (13, 14^1/$_2$, 15^1/$_2$)"/30.5 (33, 37, 39.5) cm from end of cuff (or desired length).

Back

From this point on the sleeve sts will be worked back and forth, no longer in the round.

Cont in colorwork patt as est, working even with no further shaping until back meas 8 (8, 9^1/$_4$, 9^1/$_4$)"/20.5 (20.5, 23.5, 23.5) cm from end of sleeve. End with an even (WS) row.

JOINING BACKS

Arrange sts from both sleeve/backs so that they are seated on two needles, 72 (76, 84, 88) sts on one needle, 72 (76, 84, 88) sts on the other.

continued

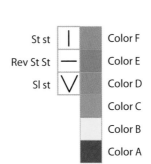

Stained Glass Armery Chart

St st	Color F
Rev St St	Color E
Sl st	Color D
	Color C
	Color B
	Color A

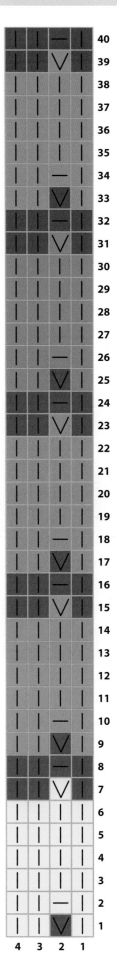

With RS of pieces facing each other and WS facing out, join both backs together with a 3-needle bind-off as follows (see page 119 for photo-illustrated instructions).

1. Place the two pieces on knitting needles so the right sides of each piece are facing each other with the needles parallel.
2. Insert a third needle one size larger through the leading edge of the first stitch on each needle (knitwise).
3. Knit these stitches together as one, leaving 1 st on RH needle.
4. Repeat steps 2–3, and slip older stitch on LH needle over newer stitch.

Repeat step 4 until all sts are bound off. Cut yarn, pull through last stitch.

NECK/SHOULDER OPENING

With smaller needle and RS facing, beg at either center back point, PU&K 224 (224, 256, 256) sts around entire Neck/Shoulder opening.

Work in St st for 2"/5 cm, then change to larger needles and cont in St st for another 2"/5 cm, or until Neck/Shoulder facing is desired length. BO all sts *loosely*.

Finishing

Weave in all ends. Steam block piece.

Finished Measurements

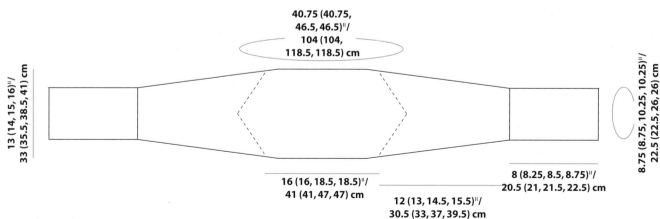

40.75 (40.75, 46.5, 46.5)"/
104 (104, 118.5, 118.5) cm

13 (14, 15, 16)"/
33 (35.5, 38.5, 41) cm

8.75 (8.75, 10.25, 10.25)"/
22.5 (22.5, 26, 26) cm

16 (16, 18.5, 18.5)"/
41 (41, 47, 47) cm

8 (8.25, 8.5, 8.75)"/
20.5 (21, 21.5, 22.5) cm

12 (13, 14.5, 15.5)"/
30.5 (33, 37, 39.5) cm

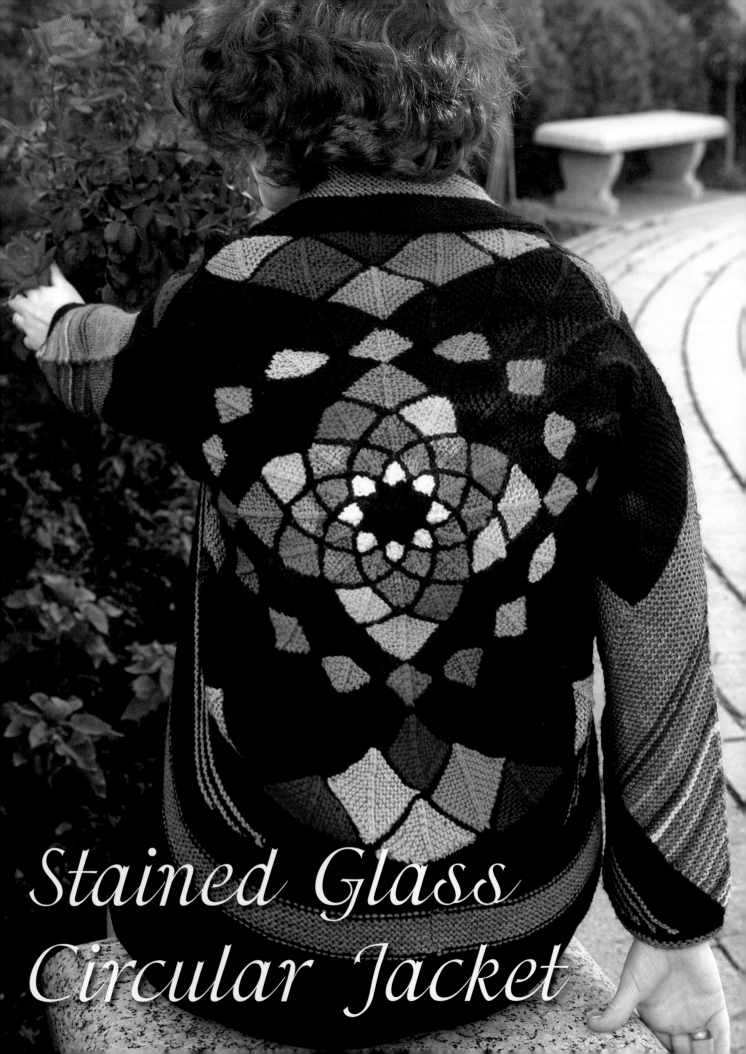

Stained Glass
Circular Jacket

This is a most unusual pattern, worked from the center out. It's almost as much sculpture as it is a hand knit pattern! The pattern is wordy, but that's because I walk you through every step. I also try to be as specific as possible for knitters at all levels.

If you want to mimic the exact colors shown in the image, see the breakdown chart of each yarn required and the total yards needed for each color (pages 85–86). Alternately, you can use odds and ends of waste yarn for some of the colors, or perhaps use a long-strand variegated yarn as a continuous contrast through the entire garment.

Sizes

Small (Medium, Large, Extra-Large)

Finished Measurements

Body circle diameter: 26^1/$_2$ (28^1/$_2$, 28^1/$_2$, 30^1/$_2$)"/67.5 (72.5, 72.5, 78) cm

Sleeve circumference: 12 (13^1/$_2$, 15^1/$_4$, 16^3/$_4$)"/30.5 (34.5, 39, 42.5) cm

Sleeve length: 10^3/$_4$ (17, 19, 21)"/27.5 (43.5, 48.5, 53.5) cm

Skill Level

Advanced

Yarn

Biggan Designs 8-ply Merino, light weight #3 yarn (100% merino; 115 yd./105 m per 1.75 oz./50 g ball)

- 7 (8, 10, 12) balls [770 (870, 1050, 1300) yd.] #000 Black (Main Color)
- 4 (4, 5, 6) balls [400 (452, 545, 675) yd.] #40 Slate [Sleeve Contrast (G1)]
- 1 (1, 1, 1) ball [115 (115, 115, 115) yd.] #495 Light Khaki [Collar Stripes (CS5)]
- 6 (7, 8, 10) balls [629 (711, 858, 1062) yd.] remaining colors (amounts combined; see chart on pages 85–86)

Needles and Other Materials

- US 5 (3.75 mm) double-pointed needles
- US 5 (3.75 mm) 48"/120 cm long circular needle
- Approx. 3 yd./3 m of waste yarn (smooth, easy to pull through stitches)
- Yarn needle

Gauge

20 sts x 28 rows in St st = 4"/10 cm square
Adjust needle size if necessary to obtain gauge.

Stitch Guide

Kfb (knit into front and back of one stitch)
Knit into the front and back of the same stitch—increase of 1 st.

PU (pick up)
Using the knitting needle only, with no source of yarn, pick up a loop from the existing fabric to create a stitch on the needle.

VDD (vertical double decrease)
Sl 2 sts as if to work k2tog-R, k1, pass slipped sts over—decrease of 2 sts.

W&T (wrap & turn)
Work the desired number of sts for the short row. Move yarn to RS. Slip next st to the right-hand needle. Move yarn to WS. Return stitch to left-hand needle. Turn and begin working back in the opposite direction.

Yarn Color Chart

In the chart below, if a color is used twice the second usage is noted in the third column. Yardages shown are the total used for each color in the entire garment. *For the second use of a color no yardage is given as it is included in the first use amount.*

Yarn ID	Color Number	Also Used For	Yardages			
			S	M	L	XL
MC	0	NE2, NE3, NW2, NW3	770	870	1050	1300
A	390		15	17	20	25
B	570		15	17	20	25
C	755		15	17	20	25
CE1	280		12	14	16	20
CE2	435	Str08	19	21	26	32
CE3	825	Str20a	16	18	22	27
CE4	380	Str07	20	23	27	34
CE5	620	F8	24	27	33	41
CE6	135	Str14	18	20	25	30
D1	270		14	16	19	24
D2	330		14	16	19	24
E1	640	Str18b	18	20	25	30
E2	510		15	17	20	25
F1	945	Str24a	11	12	15	19
F2	670		10	11	14	17
F3	955	Str24b	11	12	15	19
F4	650	S3	23	26	31	39
F5	230		10	11	14	17
F6	710	Str18a	13	15	18	22
F7	240		10	11	14	17
F8	620	CE5	—	—	—	—
G1	40		400	452	545	675
N1	905	Str21b	14	16	19	24
N2	485	Str03	21	24	29	35
N3	775	Str20b	15	17	21	25
N4	745		14	16	19	24
N5	995		14	16	19	24
N6	185	Str19b	17	19	23	29
NE1	630		14	16	19	24
NE2	0	MC	—	—	—	—
NE3	0	MC	—	—	—	—
NW1	210	Str23b	15	17	20	25
NW2	0	MC	—	—	—	—
NW3	0	MC	—	—	—	—
S1	985		12	14	16	20
S2	830	Str13	17	19	23	29
S3	650	F4	—	—	—	—
S4	220	Str23a	15	17	20	25
S5	495	Str09	115	115	115	115

Yarn Color Chart continued

Yarn ID	Color Number	Also Used For	Yardages			
			S	M	L	XL
S6	165	Str06	21	24	29	35
SE1	895	Str11	17	19	23	29
SW1	310	Str12	19	21	26	32
W1	290	Str19a	15	17	20	25
W2	465	Str22b	15	17	20	25
W3	875	Str21a	15	17	20	25
W4	610	Str01	22	25	30	37
W5	175	Str10	19	21	26	32
W6	60	Str16	17	19	23	29
Str01	610	W4	—	—	—	—
Str02	865		8	9	11	14
Str03	485	N2	—	—	—	—
Str04	455		7	8	10	12
Str05	915		7	8	10	12
Str06	165	S6	—	—	—	—
Str07	380	CE4	—	—	—	—
Str08	435	CE2	—	—	—	—
Str09	495	S5	—	—	—	—
Str10	175	W5	—	—	—	—
Str11	895	SE1	—	—	—	—
Str12	310	SW1	—	—	—	—
Str13	830	S2	—	—	—	—
Str14	135	CE6	—	—	—	—
Str15	475		4	5	5	7
Str16	60	W6	—	—	—	—
Str17	390		3	3	4	5
Str18a	710	F6	—	—	—	—
Str18b	640	E1	—	—	—	—
Str19a	290	W1	—	—	—	—
Str19b	185	N6	—	—	—	—
Str20a	825	CE3	—	—	—	—
Str20b	775	N3	—	—	—	—
Str21a	875	W3	—	—	—	—
Str21b	905	N1	—	—	—	—
Str22a	370		2	2	3	3
Str22b	465	W2	—	—	—	—
Str23a	220	S4	—	—	—	—
Str23b	210	NW1	—	—	—	—
Str24a	945	F1	—	—	—	—
Str24b	955	F3	—	—	—	—

Stained Glass Circular Jacket Schematics

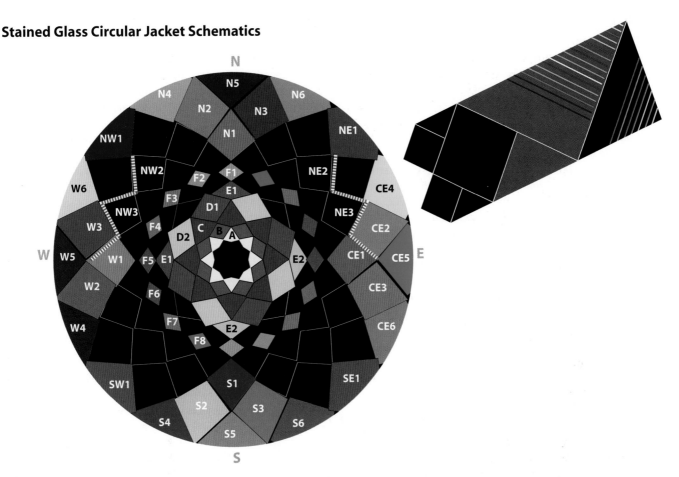

Body

With MC, CO 8 sts.

CENTER CIRCLE

Row 1: Kfb each st—16 sts.
Row 2: [Kfb, k1] 8 times—24 sts.
Divide sts onto dpns and begin working in the round.
Rnd 3 and every odd rnd: Knit all sts.
Rnd 4: [Kfb, k2] 8 times—32 sts.
Rnd 6: [Kfb, k1] 16 times—48 sts.
Rnd 8: [Kfb, k2] 16 times—64 sts.
Rnd 10 (M, L, and XL only): [Kfb, k3] 16 times—80 sts.
Rnd 12 (L and XL only): [Kfb, k4] 16 times—96 sts.
Rnd 14 (XL only): [Kfb, k5] 8 times—112 sts.
You now have a total of 64 (80, 96, 112) sts. Slip all of them onto a 48" circular needle.

MITERED BAND 1

Begin working Mitered Band 1, working each of the 8 groups in the following manner:
Row 1: With MC, k4 (5, 6, 7) sts, kfb, k3 (4, 5, 6) sts—9 (11, 13, 15) sts on needle.
Row 2 and all WS rows: K to center st, p1, k to end [in this row that would be k4 (5, 6, 7) sts, p1, k4 (5, 6, 7) sts].
Change to Color A.
Next RS row (XL only): K6, VDD, k6—13 sts rem.
Next RS row (XL and L only): K5, VDD, k5—11 sts rem.

Next RS row (XL, L, and M only): K4, VDD, k4—9 sts rem.
Next RS row (all sizes): K3, VDD, k3—7 sts rem.
Next RS row: K2, VDD, k2—5 sts rem.
Next RS row: K1, VDD, k1—3 sts rem.
Next RS row: VDD, break yarn leaving a 6"/15 cm tail, pull tail through last st.
Move on to next set of sts. Cont to next set of 8 (10, 12, 14) sts and rep the above rows to create another diamond. Work around all sts creating 8 diamonds total.

MITERED BAND 2

Beg at the tip of any diamond and with MC, PU 5 (6, 7, 8) sts down the left edge of the diamond, PU 1 st in the space between this diamond and the diamond to the left, PU 5 (6, 7, 8) sts up the right edge of the next diamond—11 (13, 15, 17) sts.
Next row and all WS rows: K to center st, p1, k to end.
Change to Color B.
Next RS row (XL only): K7, VDD, k7—15 sts rem.
Next RS row (XL and L only): K6, VDD, k6—13 sts rem.
Next RS row (XL, L, and M only): K5, VDD, k5—11 sts rem.
Next RS row (all sizes): K to 1 st before the center st, VDD, k to end—9 sts rem.
Rep last 2 rows until 3 sts rem, end with 1 final VDD, break yarn, and tie off last st.
Cont to the next valley between diamonds from Mitered Band 1. Work around all sts creating 8 diamonds total.

MITERED BAND 3

Beg at the tip of any diamond and with MC, PU 6 (7, 8, 9) sts down the left edge of the diamond, PU 1 st in the space between this diamond and the diamond to the left, PU 6 (7, 8, 9) sts up the right edge of the next diamond—13 (15, 17, 19) sts.

Next row and all WS rows: K to center st, p1, k to end. Change to Color C.

Next RS row (XL only): K8, VDD, k8—17 sts rem.

Next RS row (XL and L only): K7, VDD, k7—15 sts rem.

Next RS row (XL, L and M only): K6, VDD, k6—13 sts rem.

Next RS row (all sizes): K to 1 st before center, VDD, k to end—11 sts rem.

Rep last 2 rows until 3 sts rem, end with 1 final VDD, break yarn, and tie off last st.

Cont to the next valley between diamonds from Mitered Band 2. Work around all sts creating 8 diamonds total.

MITERED BAND 4

Beg at the tip of any diamond and with MC, PU 7 (8, 9, 10) sts down the left edge of the diamond, PU 1 st in the space between this diamond and the diamond to the left, PU 7 (8, 9, 10) sts up the right edge of the next diamond—15 (17, 19, 21) sts.

Next row and all WS rows: K to center st, p1, k to end. Change to Color D1.

Next RS row (XL only): K9, VDD, k9 —19 sts rem.

Next RS row (XL and L only): K8, VDD, k8—17 sts rem.

Next RS row (XL, L, and M only): K7, VDD, k7—15 sts rem.

Next RS row (all sizes): K to 1 st before center, VDD, k to end—13 sts rem.

Rep last 2 rows until 3 sts rem, end with 1 final VDD, break yarn, and tie off last st.

Cont to the next valley between diamonds from Mitered Band 3 and work in Color D2. Work around all sts creating 8 diamonds total, alternating diamonds in D1 and D2.

MITERED BAND 5

Beg at the tip of any diamond and with MC, PU 8 (9, 10, 11) sts down the left edge of the diamond, PU 1 st in the space between this diamond and the diamond to the left, PU 8 (9, 10, 11) sts up the right edge of the next diamond—17 (19, 21, 23) sts.

Next row and all WS rows: K to center st, p1, k to end. Change to Color E1.

Next RS row (XL only): K10, VDD, k10—21 sts rem.

Next RS row (XL and L only): K9, VDD, k9—19 sts rem.

Next RS row (XL, L, and M only): K8, VDD, k8—17 sts rem.

Next RS row (all sizes): K to 1 st before center, VDD, k to end—15 sts rem.

Rep last 2 rows until 3 sts rem, end with 1 final VDD, break yarn, and tie off last st.

Cont to the next valley between diamonds from Mitered Band 4. Work around all sts creating 8 diamonds total, alternating diamonds in E1 and E2.

MITERED BAND 6

Two-color diamonds

Beg at the tip of any diamond and with MC PU 9 (10, 11, 12) sts down the left edge of the diamond, PU 1 st in the space between this diamond and the diamond to the left, PU 9 (10, 11, 12) sts up the right edge of the next diamond—19 (21, 23, 25) sts.

Next row and all WS rows: K to center st, p1, k to end. Cont with MC.

Row 3 (RS): K8 (9, 10, 11) sts, VDD, k8 (9, 10, 11) sts—17 (19, 21, 23) sts rem.

Row 5 (RS): K to 1 st before center st, VDD, k to end.

Rep the last 2 rows 5 (5, 6, 6) times—9 (11, 11, 13) sts rem total.

Change to Color F2 and continue diamond as est.

Cont to the next valley between diamonds from Mitered Band 5, rep partial diamond using MC and Color F4. Work around all diamonds, alternating Colors F2, F4, F6, and F8 around at the tip of each diamond (use each color twice, opposite of itself in the circle).

MITERED BAND 7

With F1 and beg along the left edge of any diamond (at the point where MC meets F color) PU 4 (5, 5, 6) sts down the left edge of the diamond, PU 1 st in the space between diamonds, PU 4 (5, 5, 6) sts up the right edge to the the corresponding point—9 (11, 11, 13) sts.

Next row and all WS rows: K to center st, p1, k to end.

Cont working as for all prev diamonds, working in valleys between F2, F4, F6, and F8 diamonds alternating colors F1, F3, F5, and F7.

Create a total of 16 smaller diamonds around work in colors F1–8, each with a base of 9 (11, 11, 13) sts.

MITERED BAND 8

Beg at the tip of any diamond and with MC, PU 5 (6, 7, 8) sts down the left edge of the diamond, PU 1 st in the space between this diamond and the diamond to the left, PU 5 (6, 7, 8) sts up the right edge of the next diamond—11 (13, 15, 17) sts.

Next row and all WS rows: K to center st, p1, k to end. Cont with MC only;

Next RS row (XL only): K7, VDD, k7—15 sts rem.

Next RS row (XL and L only): K6, VDD, k6—13 sts rem.

Next RS row (XL, L, and M only): K5, VDD, k5—11 sts rem.

Next RS row (all sizes): K to 1 st before center, VDD, k to end—9 sts rem.

Rep last 2 rows until 3 sts rem, end with 1 final VDD, break yarn, and tie off last st.

Cont to the next valley between diamonds from Mitered Band 7. Work around all sts creating 8 diamonds total.

Radiating from the center point of the work are four lines, like compass points.

Label these points N, S, E, and W (see schematic). This is how they'll be referred to in the pattern from this point on.

MITERED BAND 9
Initial Compass Points

Beg at V at the North point of the compass and with MC, PU
6 (7, 8, 9) sts down the left edge of the diamond, PU 1 st
in the space between this diamond and the diamond to
the left, PU 6 (7, 8, 9) sts up the right edge of the next diamond—13 (15, 17, 19) sts.

Next row and all WS rows: K to center st, p1, k to end.
Cont with Color N1.
Next RS row (XL only): K8, VDD, k8—17 sts rem.
Next RS row (XL and L only): K7, VDD, k7—15 sts rem.
Next RS row (XL, L, and M only): K6, VDD, k6—13 sts rem.
Next RS row (all sizes): K5, VDD, k5—11 sts rem.
Cont as with and finish as with previous diamonds.
Move to the V at the South point and work the above dia-
mond using color S1.
Repeat at the East and West points with colors CE1 and W1.
Create a diamond in each remaining V in this band with MC
only—16 diamonds total.

Mark Armhole

Look at the schematic and note the wide red zigzag lines.
These are the armhole openings and will be marked with
waste yarn.
With a piece of waste yarn and beg at the tip of the East
diamond, PU 7 (8, 9, 10) sts along the left edge of that
diamond, PU 1 in the center of the V.

Continuing, PU 14 (16, 18, 20) sts up the right edge, then
down the left edge of the next diamond, PU 1 in the center of the next V.
Finally PU 7 (8, 9, 10) sts up the left edge of the next diamond—30 (34, 38, 42) sts total on waste yarn.
Leave waste yarn and repeat at opposite side of the garment, beginning at the NW point and working in the
same manner to the tip at the westernmost diamond.

MITERED BAND 10

Beg at the tip of the North diamond and with MC, PU 7 (8,
9, 10) sts down the left edge of the diamond, PU 1 st in
the space between this diamond and the diamond to the
left, PU 7 (8, 9, 10) sts up the right edge of the next diamond—15 (17, 19, 21) sts.

Next row and all WS rows: K to center st, p1, k to end.
Cont with Color N2 only.
Next RS row (XL only): K9, VDD, k9—19 sts rem.
Next RS row (XL and L only): K8, VDD, k8—17 sts rem.
Next RS row (XL, L, and M only): K7, VDD, k7—15 sts rem.
Next RS row (all sizes): K to 1 st before center, VDD, k to
end—13 sts rem.
Rep last 2 rows until 3 sts rem, end with 1 final VDD, break
yarn, and tie off last st.
Repeat the above directions on the opposite edge of the
North diamond using MC and Color N3.

continued

Repeat the above 2 diamonds at the East, West, and South diamonds using MC and Colors CE1 and CE2, W1 and W2, S1 and S2 on either side of their respective compass point diamonds.

Create a diamond in each remaining V in this band with MC only—16 diamonds total.

MITERED BAND 11
Partial Edge Diamonds

Beg at V opening at the North point of the compass and with MC, PU 8 (9, 10, 11) sts down the left edge of the diamond, PU 1 st in the space between this diamond and the diamond to the left, PU 8 (9, 10, 11) sts up the right edge of the next diamond—17 (19, 21, 23) sts.

Next row (WS): K to center st, p1, k to the end of the row. Cont with Color N5.

Next row *(M and XL only)*: K0 (8, 0, 10) sts, VDD, k0 (8, 0, 10) sts, turn work—17 (17, 21, 21) sts.

Next row and all WS rows: K to center st, p1, k to the end of the row.

Next row (RS): K7 (7, 9, 9) sts, VDD, k6 (6, 8, 8) sts, wrap yarn around next stitch and turn work (W&T).

Next row (WS): K6 (6, 8, 8) sts, p1, k6 (6, 8, 8) sts, W&T.

Next row (RS): K5 (5, 7, 7) sts, VDD, k4 (4, 6, 6) sts, W&T.

Next row (WS): K4 (4, 6, 6) sts, p1, k4 (4, 6, 6) sts, W&T.

Next row (RS): K3 (3, 5, 5) sts, VDD, k2 (2, 4, 4) sts, W&T.

Next row (WS): K2 (2, 4, 4) sts, p1, k2 (2, 4, 4) sts, W&T.

Next row (RS): K1 (1, 3, 3) sts, VDD, k0 (0, 2, 2) sts, W&T.

Next row (WS): K0 (0, 2, 2) sts, p1, k to end of diamond, slipping wraps up onto needle and working along with each wrapped st—9 (9, 13, 13) sts.

Next row *(S and L only)*: Knit all sts.

Next row *(M and XL only)*: K1, kfb, k to last 2 sts in diamond, kfb, k1—9 (11, 13, 15) sts.

Continuing with the next V opening to the left and working with MC and Color N4, create a flattened diamond as above.

Leaving the rem 9 (11, 13, 15) sts from each flattened diamond on the circ needles, continue working leftward around edge, working in the following colors (in order): NW1, W6, W5, W4, SW1, S6, S5, S4, SE1, CE6, CE5, CE4, NE1, N6.

At this point there should be 144 (176, 208, 240) sts total on the needle.

Facing/Collar

Arrange sts so you're ready to begin working at the center bottom (South point on the compass).

Next rnd: With MC [k9 (11, 13, 15) sts, place marker (pm)] 16 times. Do not use the contrasting marker at this point.

Next rnd: Purl all sts, slipping markers.

BEGIN SHORT-ROW SHAPING

Next 2 rows: Knit all sts, slipping markers, until 3 sts rem at end of round unworked, W&T.

Rows 1 and 3 (RS): Knit all sts until 3 sts rem before W&T from last RS row, W&T.

Row 2 (WS): Knit all sts, inc 1 st in every section, placed randomly. Work to 3 sts before W&T from last WS row.

Row 4 (WS): Knit all sts until 3 sts rem before W&T from last WS row.

Rep last 4 rows three times more, working an inc in each rep of Row 2, and placing increases randomly. Do not increase in any section which contains less than 4 sts—there will be 13 (15, 17, 19) sts in widest sections.

From this point total stitch counts will not be given for the body edge, just stitch counts for the widest sections.

TRIPLE STRIPE SECTION

Continuing in Short Row Shaping as est, and working an inc in each rep of Row 2 as est, change colors as foll:

[Work 2 rows in S5, work 2 rows in MC] three times—16 (18, 20, 22) sts in the widest sections near the top of the body.

Add a contrasting marker at the the current point to mark the new start of round.

FACING SHAPING

Rnd 1: Knit all sts.

Rnds 2 and 4: Purl all sts in round.

Rnd 3: [Knit to next marker, inc 1 st anywhere in the current segment] 16 times—17 (19, 21, 23) sts in widest sections.

Work last 4 rounds three times more, then work Rnd 1 once more—20 (22, 24, 26) sts in widest sections.

SINGLE WIDE STRIPE SECTION

Next rnd: With G1, purl all sts.

Next rnd: With G1, knit all sts.

Rep last 2 rnds six times, increasing every 4 rnds as est (14 rounds of G1 total)—24 (26, 28, 30) sts in widest sections.

Next rnd: With MC, purl all sts.

Next rnd: With MC, knit all sts.

Rep last 2 rnds eight times, increasing every 4 rnds as est—28 (30, 32, 34) sts in widest sections.

Bind off all sts [approx 448 (480, 512, 544) sts] loosely with MC.

Sleeve (Make 2, Following Appropriate Left/Right Chart)

Return to the waste yarn marking the Armhole.

Carefully remove waste yarn, slipping the 30 (34, 38, 42) sts from the top of the armhole (front of sleeve) onto circular needle. Set aside to work later.

Dealing with the bottom (Back) sts only, which will have a firm edge, there should be two obvious V areas. Two diamonds will be worked in these areas. See the Sleeve chart for clarification.

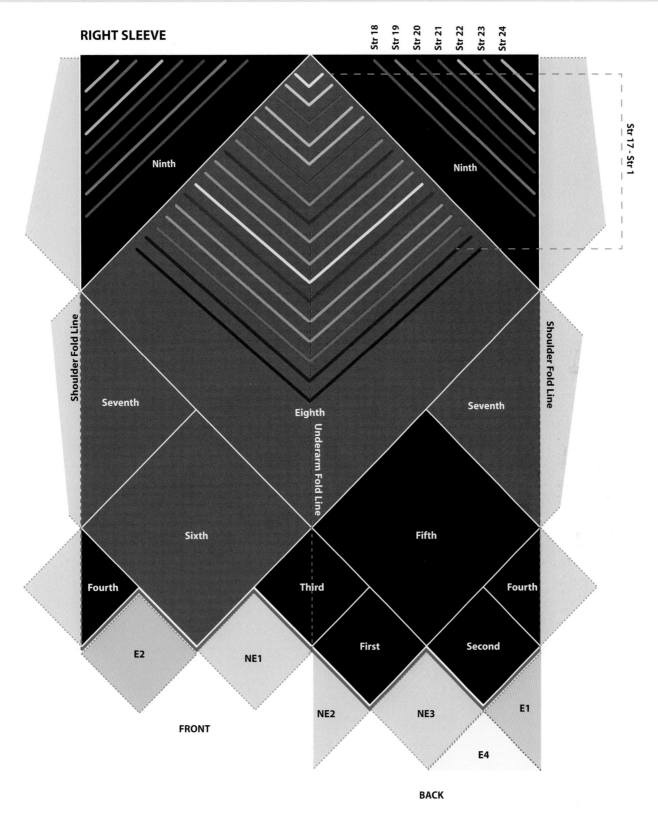

RIGHT SLEEVE

Str 18 Str 19 Str 20 Str 21 Str 22 Str 23 Str 24

Str 17 - Str 1

Ninth

Ninth

Shoulder Fold Line

Shoulder Fold Line

Seventh

Eighth

Seventh

Underarm Fold Line

Sixth

Fifth

Fourth

Third

Fourth

E2

NE1

First

Second

E1

NE2

NE3

E4

FRONT

BACK

FIRST SLEEVE DIAMOND

Beg at the tip of the diamond in the center of the sleeve
bottom, with MC PU 7 (8, 9, 10) sts down the left edge of
the diamond, PU 1 at the bottom of the V, PU 7 (8, 9, 10)
sts up the right edge of the next diamond—15 (17, 19,
21) sts.

Next row and all WS rows: K to center st, p1, k to end.

Next row (RS): K6 (7, 8, 9) sts, VDD, k6 (7, 8, 9) sts—15 (17,
19, 21) sts rem.

Next row and all WS rows: K to center st, p1, k to end.

Cont as est, dec at center of every RS row as with body until
3 sts rem, end with 1 final VDD, break yarn and tie off
last st.

LEFT SLEEVE

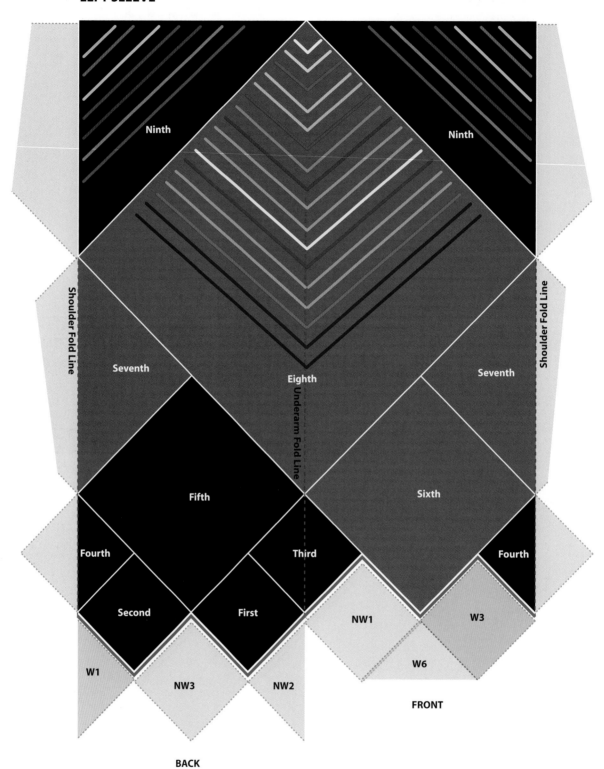

SECOND SLEEVE DIAMOND

Repeat the above diamond in the remaining V space at the Back armhole.

THIRD SLEEVE DIAMOND

Note: The Third and Fourth Diamonds will be worked at either side of the First and Second Diamonds, straddling the line from front to back of sleeve.

Beg at the tip of the First Sleeve Diamond, with MC PU 7 (8, 9, 10) sts down the left edge of the First Sleeve Diamond, then PU 1 st at the point where the First Diamond meets the armhole, then K7 (8, 9, 10) live sts up to the first point at the armhole front—15 (17, 19, 21) sts.

Work Third Diamond in the same manner as the First and Second Diamonds.

FOURTH SLEEVE DIAMOND

Leaving the 15 sts at the center of the armhole front live, with MC k7 (8, 9, 10) sts down the left edge of the second point, PU 1 st at the point where the armhole meets the Second Diamond, then PU 7 (8, 9, 10) sts up the right edge of the Second Diamond—15 (17, 19, 21) sts.

Work Fourth Diamond in the same manner as the Third Diamond.

FIFTH SLEEVE DIAMOND

The Fifth Diamond is twice the size of the diamonds previously worked in the sleeve.

Beg at the tip of the Fourth Diamond, with MC PU 15 (17, 19, 21) sts down the left edges of the Fourth and Second Diamonds, PU 1 st in the valley from the armhole back, PU 15 (17, 19, 21) sts up along the First and Third Diamond Edges—31 (35, 39, 43) sts.

Working in the same manner as with the previous diamonds, work this larger diamond by decreasing 2 sts in a VDD in the center of every RS row, working the WS rows by knitting to the center st, p1, knit to the end.

SIXTH SLEEVE DIAMOND

Note: The Sixth Diamond is the first sleeve diamond worked in Color G1.

Beg at the tip of the Third Diamond, with G1 PU 7 (8, 9, 10) sts down the left edges of the Fourth diamond, work 8 (9, 10, 11) live sts to the center of the V, PU 1 st in the valley from the armhole front, work 8 (9, 10, 11) live sts up the left edge of the V, PU 7 (8, 9, 10) sts up along the First and Third Diamond Edges—31 (35, 39, 43) sts.

Work Sixth Diamond in the same manner as the Fifth Diamond.

SEVENTH SLEEVE DIAMOND

Beg at the tip of the Sixth Diamond, with G1 PU 15 (17, 19, 21) sts down the left edges of the Sixth Diamond, PU 1 st in the center of the V, PU 15 (17, 19, 21) sts up along the Fifth Diamond Edge—31 (35, 39, 43) sts.

Work Seventh Diamond in the same manner as the Sixth Diamond.

EIGHTH SLEEVE DIAMOND

Beg at the tip of the Seventh Diamond, with Color G1 PU 15 (17, 19, 21) sts down the left edges of the Seventh Diamond, continuing in the same direction, PU 15 (17, 19, 21) sts down the left side of the Fifth Diamond [30 (34, 38, 42) sts total], PU 1 st in the center of the V, PU 30 (34, 38, 42) sts up along the Sixth Diamond Edge and the right edge of the Seventh Diamond—61 (69, 77, 85) sts.

Work Eighth Diamond in the same manner as previous diamonds until 24 rows (12 garter ridges) have been worked.

Cont decreasing as est, work stripe motif as foll:

Stripe

Row 1 (RS): With Color Str01, k to 1 st before center st, VDD, k to end of row.

Row 2 (WS): Cont with Color Str01, k to center st, p1, k to end of row.

Row 3 (RS): With Color G1, k to 1 st before center st, VDD, k to end of row.

Row 4 (WS): Cont with Color G1, k to center st, p1, k to end of row.

Cont in this manner, using Colors Str02—Str17 until a total of 17 stripes have been worked (there will be a gray ridge between each colored stripe). Finish the diamond with Color G1 only.

NINTH SLEEVE DIAMOND

Beg at the tip of the Eighth Diamond and with MC, PU 30 (34, 38, 42) sts down the left edge of the Eighth Diamond, PU 1 st in the center of the V, PU 30 (34, 38, 42) sts up the right edge of the Eighth Diamond—61 (69, 77, 85) sts.

Next row (WS): K to center st, p1, k to the end of the row.

Next row (RS): K29 (33, 37, 41) sts, VDD, k28 (32, 36, 40) sts, wrap yarn around next stitch and turn work (W&T)—58 (66, 74, 82) sts rem.

Next row (WS): K28 (32, 36, 40) sts, p1, k28 (32, 36, 40) sts, W&T.

Next row (RS): K27 (31, 35, 39) sts, VDD, k26 (30, 34, 38) sts, wrap yarn around next stitch and turn work (W&T)—54 (62, 70, 78) sts rem.

Next row (WS): K26 (30, 34, 38) sts, p1, k26 (30, 34, 38) sts, W&T.

Next row (RS): K to 1 st before center st, VDD, k to 1 st before wrapped st from prev RS row, W&T.

Next row (WS): K to center st, p1, k to 1 st before wrapped st from prev WS row, W&T.

Rep last 2 rows until a total of 18 rows (9 garter ridges) have been worked.

Cont with short row shaping and decreasing at the center as est, creating stripes as foll:

Stripe

Row 1 (RS): With Color Str18a, k to 1 st before center st, VDD, k to 1 st before wrapped st from prev RS row.

Row 2 (WS): With Color Str18b, k to center st, p1, k to 1 st before wrapped st from prev WS row, W&T.

Row 3 (RS): With Color G1, k to 1 st before center st, VDD, k to 1 st before wrapped st from prev RS row.

Row 4 (WS): K to center st, p1, k to 1 st before wrapped st from prev WS row, W&T.

Cont in this manner, using Colors Str19a—Str24b until a total of 6 stripes have been worked, each stripe comprised of two colors (a and b) with a black ridge between each colored stripe. Finish the diamond with Color G1 only and *at the same time* continue working short rows and decreasing as est until all sts have been wrapped, 29 (33, 37, 41) sts rem on needle total.

Next rnd (RS): K to the end of the round, slipping wraps up onto needle and working along with each wrapped st, place marker to note start of round.

Next rnd: Purl to the end of the round.

The last st wrapped should be the stitch immediately to the right of the center stitch. Depending on the size you're working, you may or may not have one final VDD to work in the last RS row.

Try on the jacket and determine the desired sleeve length. Continue with G1 or MC, whichever you prefer, working even with no further shaping until sleeve is desired length. Bind off all sts loosely.

Finishing

Weave in remaining ends. Steam block piece.

Schematic and Finished Measurements

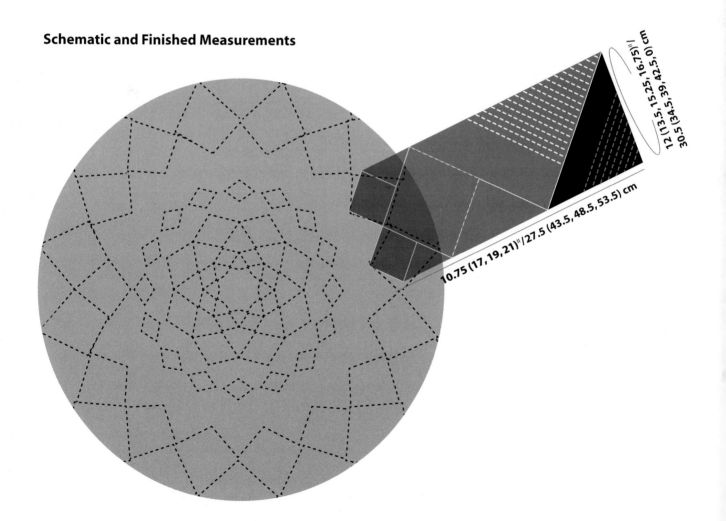

12 (13.5, 15.25, 16.75)" / 30.5 (34.5, 39, 42.5, 0) cm

10.75 (17, 19, 21)" / 27.5 (43.5, 48.5, 53.5) cm

Strasbourg Cape

Inspired by the Rose Window in the Strasbourg Cathedral, this shawl features six panels, a collar, and a lace edge at the bottom. The color sections are worked in a simple lace with an arching, gothic motif. The dark tracery lines are created using long individual strands of a contrasting semi-solid yarn.

Sizes
One Size

Finished Measurements
Length: 19$\frac{1}{2}$"/50 cm
Lower edge circumference: 86"/218 cm

Skill Level
Advanced

Yarn
Kauni Effekt, super fine #1 yarn (100% wool; 439 yd./400 m per 3.5 oz./100 g ball)
• 1 ball EQ Rainbow (MC)
Regia Racing Stripes, super fine #1 yarn (75% wool, 25% nylon; 460 yd./420 m per 3.5 oz./100 g ball)
• 1 ball #0887 Charcoal/Black (CC)

Needles and Other Materials
• US 5 (3.75 mm) 40"/100 cm long circular needle
• Waste yarn
• 6 stitch markers
• 5 safety pins
• Yarn needle

Gauge
20 sts x 28 rows in charted Lace patt = 4"/10 cm square
Adjust needle size if necessary to obtain gauge.

Stitch Guide

K2tog-L (knit 2 tog with a left slant)
Knit 2 stitches together so the working needle is pointing to the left as it enters the stitch (dec will slant to the left); common left-slanting decreases are ssk, k2tog-tbl, or skp.

K2tog-R (knit 2 tog with a right slant)
Knit 2 stitches together so the working needle is pointing to the right as it enters the stitch (dec will slant to the right); most common is k2tog.

K3tog-L (knit 3 tog with a left slant)
Knit 3 sts together so the working needle is pointing to the left as it enters the stitch (dec will slant to the left); common decreases are sssk, k3togTBL, or sl2, k1, psso.

K3tog-R (knit 3 tog with a right slant)
Knit 3 sts together so the working needle is pointing to the right as it enters the stitch (dec will slant to the right); most common is k3tog.

PU (pick up)
Using the knitting needle only, with no source of yarn, pick up a loop from the existing fabric to create a stitch on the needle.

VDD (vertical double decrease)
Sl 2 sts as if to work k2tog-R, k1, pass slipped sts over— decrease of 2 sts.

VDI (vertical double increase)
K into front of st, yo, k into back of same stitch.

VQD (vertical quad decrease)
Sl 3 sts as if to work k3tog-R, k2tog-L, pass slipped sts over knit st—decrease of 4 sts.

W&T (wrap & turn)
Work the desired number of sts for the short row. Move yarn to RS. Slip next st to the right-hand needle. Move yarn to WS. Return stitch to left-hand needle. Turn and begin working back in the opposite direction.

TIP: To keep the CC strands from becoming unworkably tangled, create six small balls (approx. 20 yd./18 m each) of contrasting color (CC). Safety pin these to the wrong side of the work, each placed at its individual color change.

Work to the CC strand, cross the strands to work the 4 CC sts as charted, then uncross the strands (thus releasing the CC strand) and continue to the next dark tracery line with very little tangling. Use the ball of yarn for the first CC section, at the edge, as this will be used for the garter rows of CC which run between the charted sections.

It will be easier to use the above technique after there is over an inch of fabric on the needles, but once you're able to pin the balls to the WS of the work, it will make this a much quicker knit!

Cape

Before you cast on, create six small balls (approximately 20 yd./18 m each) of CC, set aside.

With large skein of CC and a piece of waste yarn, and using any provisional cast-on technique, CO 22 sts.

WORK SECTION 1 CHART

K2, sm, work Section 1 chart six times across work, end k2, as foll:

Row 1: K2, pm, [k1, VDI, k1, pm] six times, k2—34 sts.

All WS rows: Knit the CC sts, purl the MC sts across the row.

Row 3: K2, sm, [k2, VDI, k2, sm] six times, k2—46 sts.

Row 5: With CC k2, sm, [k1, with MC k5, with CC k1, sm] six times, using a new 20-yard ball of CC for each repeat, end k2 in CC. The larger ball of CC should remain at the beginning of the row.

Row 7: With CC k2, sm, [k1, with MC k2, yo, k1, yo, k2, with CC k1, sm] six times, with CC k2.

Row 9: With CC k2, sm, [k1, with MC k3, yo, k1, yo, k3, with CC k1, sm] six times, with CC k2.

Row 11: With CC k2, sm, [k1, with MC k4, yo, k1, yo, k4, with CC k1, sm] six times, with CC k2.

Row 13: With CC k2, sm, [k1, with MC k4, yo, k3, yo, k4, with CC k1, sm] six times, with CC k2.

Row 15: With CC k2, sm, [k1, with MC k4, yo, k1, yo, VDD, yo, k1, yo, k4, with CC k1, sm] six times, with CC k2.

Row 17: With CC k2, sm, [k1, with MC k2, K2tog-R, yo, k2, yo, VDD, yo, k2, yo, k2tog-L, k2, with CC k1, sm] six times, with CC k2.

Row 19: With CC k2, sm, [k1, with MC k1, K2tog-R, yo, k3, yo, VDD, yo, k3, yo, k2tog-L, k1, with CC k1, sm] six times, with CC k2.

Rows 21–22: With large skein of CC only, knit 2 rows (creating 2 rows of garter).

Section 1 Chart

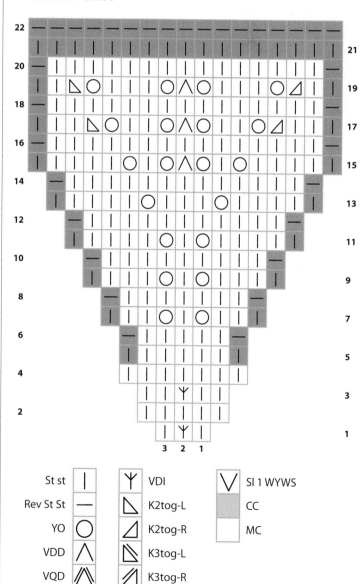

St st	│	Ⅴ VDI	SI 1 WYWS
Rev St St	─	K2tog-L	CC
YO	O	K2tog-R	MC
VDD	∧	K3tog-L	
VQD	∧∧	K3tog-R	

Section 2 Chart

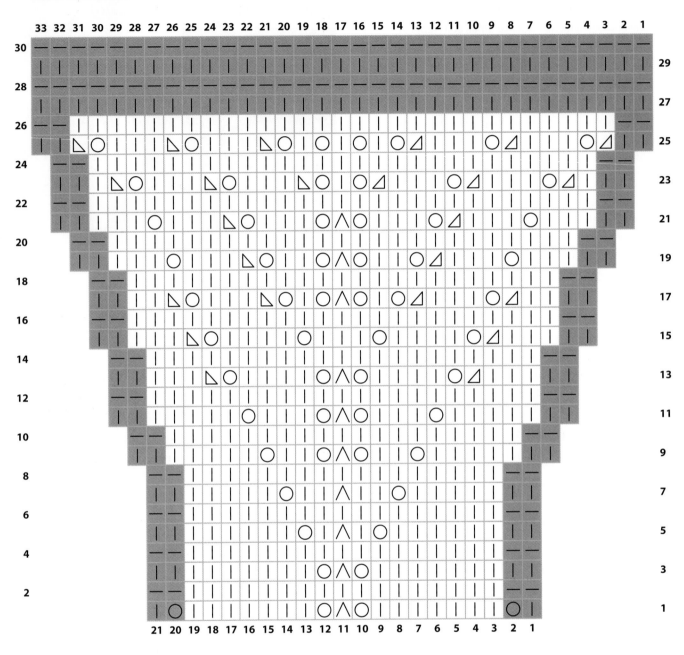

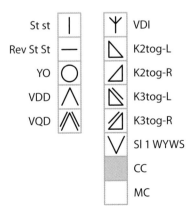

	St st				VDI
	Rev St St	—			K2tog-L
	YO	○			K2tog-R
	VDD	∧			K3tog-L
	VQD	⋀			K3tog-R
					Sl 1 WYWS
					CC
					MC

WORK SECTION 2 CHART

Working as for Section 1 Chart, use a separate yarn source for each CC area. Note that in Row 1 of Section 2 chart, sts are increased in each MC section *and* in each CC section, making 4 CC sts total between each MC area, and 3 CC sts at each edge.

Row 1: With CC k2, sm, [k1, yo, with MC k7, yo, VDD, yo, k7, with CC yo, k1, sm] six times, with CC k2.

Row 2 and all WS rows: Knit the CC sts, purl the MC sts across the row.

Row 3: With CC k2, sm, [k2, with MC k7, yo, VDD, yo, k7, with CC k2, sm] six times, with CC k2.

Row 5: With CC k2, sm, [k2, with MC k6, yo, k1, VDD, k1, yo, k6, with CC k2, sm] six times, with CC k2.

Row 7: With CC k2, sm, [k2, with MC k5, yo, k2, VDD, k2, yo, k5, with CC k2, sm] six times, with CC k2.

Row 9: With CC k2, sm, [k2, with MC k5, yo, k2, yo, VDD, yo, k2, yo, k5, with CC k2, sm] six times, with CC k2.

Row 11: With CC k2, sm, [k2, with MC k5, yo, k3, yo, VDD, yo, k3, yo, k5, with CC k2, sm] six times, with CC k2.

Row 13: With CC k2, sm, [k2, with MC k3, k2tog-R, yo, k4, yo, VDD, yo, k4, yo, k2tog-L, k3, with CC k2, sm] six times, with CC k2.

Row 15: With CC k2, sm, [k2, with MC k3, k2tog-R, yo, k4, k3, yo, k4, yo, k2tog-L, k3, with CC k2, sm] six times, with CC k2.

Row 17: With CC k2, sm, [k2, with MC k2, k2tog-R, yo, k3, k2tog-R, yo, k1, yo, VDD, yo, k1, yo, k2tog-L, k3, yo, k2tog-L, k2, with CC k2, sm] six times, with CC k2.

Row 19: With CC k2, sm, [k2, with MC k3, yo, k3, k2tog-R, yo, k2, yo, VDD, yo, k2, yo, k2tog-L, k3, yo, k3, with CC k2, sm] six times, with CC k2.

Row 21: With CC k2, sm, [k2, with MC k3, yo, k3, k2tog-R, yo, k3, yo, VDD, yo, k3, yo, k2tog-L, k3, yo, k3, with CC k2, sm] six times, with CC k2.

Row 23: With CC k2, sm, [k2, with MC k1, (k2tog-R, yo, k3) twice, k2tog-R, yo, k1, (yo, k2tog-L, k3) twice, yo, k2tog-L, k1 with CC k2, sm] six times, with CC k2.

Row 25: With CC k2, sm, [k2, with MC (k2tog-R, yo, k3) twice, k2tog-R, yo, (k1, yo) twice, k1 (yo, k2tog-L, k3) twice, yo, k2tog-L, with CC k2, sm] six times, with CC k2.

Rows 27–30: With large skein of CC only, knit 4 rows (creating 4 rows of garter).

WORK SECTION 3 CHART

Follow chart for Section 3 as established in Section 2.

Row 1: With CC k2, sm, [k2, with MC k5, yo, k3tog-R, yo, k2, yo, k2tog-R, yo, k1, VDD, k1, yo, k2tog-L, yo, k2, yo, k3tog-L, yo, k5, with CC k2, sm] six times, with CC k2.

Row 2 and all WS rows: Knit the CC sts, purl the MC sts across the row.

Row 3: With CC k2, sm, [k2, with MC k4, yo, k3tog-R, yo, k3, yo, k2tog-R, yo, k1, yo, VDD, yo, k1, yo, k2tog-L, yo, k3, yo, k3tog-L, yo, k4, with CC k2, sm] six times, with CC k2.

Row 5: With CC k2, sm, [k2, with MC k3, yo, k3tog-R, yo, k4, yo, k2tog-R, yo, k2, yo, VDD, yo, k2, yo, k2tog-L, yo, k4, yo, k3tog-L, yo, k3, with CC k2, sm] six times, with CC k2.

Row 7: With CC k2, sm, [k2, with MC k2, yo, k3tog-R, yo, k5, yo, k2tog-R, yo, k1, k2tog-R, yo, VDD, yo, k2tog-L, k1, yo, k2tog-L, yo, k5, yo, k3tog-L, yo, k2, with CC k2, sm] six times, with CC k2.

Row 9: With CC k2, sm, [k2, with MC k1, yo, k3tog-R, yo, k1, (yo, k2tog-L) twice, k1, yo, k2tog-R, yo, k1, k2tog-R, yo, k3, yo, k2tog-L, k1, yo, k2tog-L, yo, k1, (k2tog-R, yo) twice, k1, yo, k3tog-L, yo, k1, with CC k2, sm] six times, with CC k2.

Row 11: With CC k2, sm, [k2, with MC yo, k3tog-R, yo, k3, (yo, k2tog-L) twice, yo, k2tog-R, yo, k1, k2tog-R, yo, k1, yo, VDD, yo, k1, yo, k2tog-L, k1, yo, k2tog-L, yo, (k2tog-R, yo) twice, k3, yo, k3tog-L, yo, with CC k2, sm] six times, with CC k2.

Rows 13–16: With large skein of CC only, knit 4 rows (creating 4 rows of garter).

WORK SECTION 4 CHART

Follow chart for Section 4 as established—310 sts total at end of Section 4.

Row 1: With CC k2, sm, [k2, with MC k1, yo, k3tog-L, yo, k6, yo, k3tog-R, yo, k2, yo, k2tog-L, yo, k3, yo, k2tog-L, yo, k2, yo, k3tog-L, yo, k6, yo, k3tog-R, yo, k1, with CC k2, sm] six times, with CC k2.

Row 2 and all WS rows: Knit the CC sts, purl the MC sts across the row.

Row 3: With CC k2, sm, [k2, with MC k2, yo, k3tog-L, yo, k4, yo, k3tog-R, yo, k3, yo, k2tog-R, yo, k1, yo, VDD, yo, k1, yo, k2tog-L, yo, k3, yo, k3tog-L, yo, k4, yo, k3tog-R, yo, k2, with CC k2, sm] six times, with CC k2.

Row 5: With CC k2, sm, [k2, with MC k3, yo, k3tog-L, yo, k2, yo, k3tog-R, yo, k4, yo, k2tog-R, yo, k2, VDD, k2, yo, k2tog-L, yo, k4, yo, k3tog-L, yo, k2, yo, k3tog-R, yo, k3, with CC k2, sm] six times, with CC k2.

Row 7: With CC k2, sm, [k2, with MC k1, yo, k3, yo, k3tog-L, yo, k3tog-R, yo, k5, yo, k2tog-R, yo, k2, yo, VDD, yo, k2, yo, k2tog-L, yo, k5, yo, k3tog-L, yo, k3tog-R, yo, k3, yo, k1, with CC k2, sm] six times, with CC k2.

Row 9: With CC k2, sm, [k2, with MC k2, yo, k2tog-L, k2, yo, VDD, yo, k6, yo, k2tog-R, yo, k3, yo, VDD, yo, k3, yo, k2tog-L, yo, k6, yo, VDD, yo, k2, k2tog-R, yo, k2, with CC k2, sm] six times, with CC k2.

Row 11: With CC k2, sm, [k2, with MC k3, yo, k2tog-L, yo, k1, yo, VDD, yo, k6, yo, k2tog-R, yo, k3, VQD, k3, yo, k2tog-L, yo, k6, yo, VDD, yo, k1, yo, k2tog-R, yo, k3, with CC k2, sm] six times, with CC k2.

Row 13: With CC k2, sm, [k2, with MC k2, yo, k2, yo, k2tog-L, yo, k1, yo, VDD, yo, k6, yo, k2tog-R, yo, k2, VQD, k2, yo, k2tog-L, yo, k6, yo, VDD, yo, k1, yo, k2tog-R, yo, k2, yo, k2, with CC k2, sm] six times, with CC k2.

Row 15: With CC k2, sm, [k2, with MC k3, yo, k2tog-L, k1, yo, k2tog-L, k1, yo, VDD, yo, k6, yo, k2tog-R, yo, k2, VDD, k2, yo, k2tog-L, yo, k6, yo, VDD, yo, k1, k2tog-R, yo, k1, k2tog-R, yo, k3, with CC k2, sm] six times, with CC k2.

Rows 17–20: With large skein of CC only, knit 4 rows (creating 4 rows of garter).

Section 3 Chart

Y	VDI	
△	K2tog-L	
◁	K2tog-R	
◪	K3tog-L	
◩	K3tog-R	
V	Sl 1 WYWS	
▨	CC	
☐	MC	

│	St st	
—	Rev St St	
○	YO	
<	VDD	
≪	VQD	

Section 4 Chart

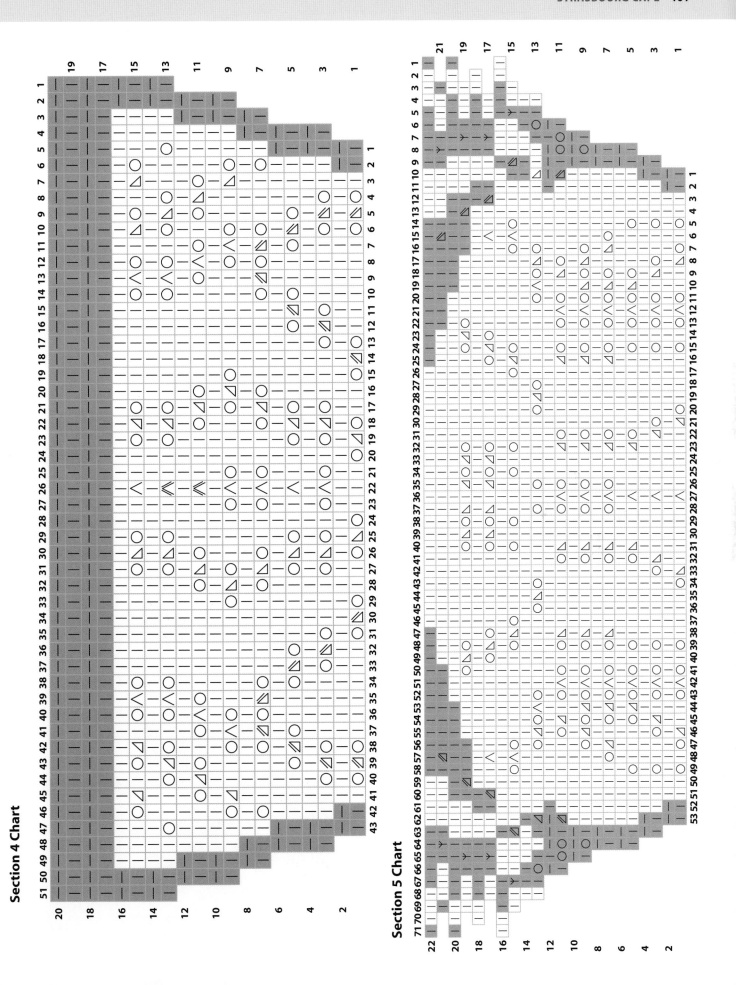

Section 5 Chart

WORK SECTION 5 CHART

Row 1: With CC k2, sm, [k2, with MC k2, yo, k1, yo, k2tog-L, k2, yo, VDD, yo, k1, yo, k4, yo, k2tog-R, k5, VDD, k5, k2tog-L, yo, k4, yo, k1, yo, VDD, yo, k2, k2tog-R, yo, k1, yo, k2, with CC k2, sm] six times, with CC k2.

Row 2 and all WS rows to Row 12: Knit the CC sts, purl the MC sts across the row.

Row 3: With CC k2, sm, [k2, with MC k3, yo, k2, yo, k2tog-L, k1, yo, VDD, yo, k1, yo, k5, yo, k2tog-R, k4, VDD, k4, k2tog-L, yo, k5, yo, k1, yo, VDD, yo, k1, k2tog-R, yo, k2, yo, k3, with CC k2, sm] six times, with CC k2.

Row 5: With CC k2, sm, [k2, with MC k4, yo, k3, yo, k2tog-L, yo, VDD, yo, k1, yo, k6, yo, k2tog-R, k3, VDD, k3, k2tog-L, yo, k6, yo, k1, yo, VDD, yo, k2tog-R, yo, k3, yo, k4, with CC k2, sm] six times, with CC k2.

Row 7: With CC k2, sm, [k2, with MC k5, yo, k2tog-L, k1, yo, k2tog-L, yo, VDD, yo, k1, yo, k2tog-R, k5, yo, k2tog-R, k2, yo, VDD, yo, k2, k2tog-L, yo, k5, k2tog-L, yo, k1, yo, VDD, yo, k2tog-R, yo, k1, k2tog-L, yo, k5, with CC k2, sm] six times, with CC k2.

Row 9: With CC k2, sm, [k1, yo, k1, with MC k6, (yo, k2tog-L) twice, yo, VDD, yo, k1, yo, k2tog-R, k5, yo, k2tog-R, k2, yo, VDD, yo, k2, k2tog-L, yo, k5, k2tog-L, yo, k1, yo, VDD, yo, k2tog-R, yo, k2tog-R, yo, k6, with CC k1, yo, k1, sm] six times, with CC k2.

Row 11: With CC k2, sm, [k1, yo, yo, k1, k3tog-L, with MC k6, yo, k2tog-L, k1, yo, VDD, yo, k1, yo, k2tog-R, k5, yo, k2tog-R, k2, yo, VDD, yo, k2, k2tog-L, yo, k5, k2tog-L, yo, k1, yo, VDD, yo, k1, k2tog-R, yo, k6, with CC k3tog-R, k1, yo, yo, k1, sm] six times, with CC k2.

Row 12 (WS): With CC k2, sm, [k1, p1, k3, p1, with MC purl to last 6 sts in section, with CC p1, k3, p1, k1, sm] six times, with CC k2.

Row 13: With CC k2, sm, [with MC, k1, with CC k1, yo, k1, with MC k2, k2tog-L, k5, yo, k2tog-L, yo, VDD, yo, k6, yo, k2tog-R, yo, k5, yo, k1, yo, k5, yo, k2tog-L, yo, k6, yo, VDD, yo, k2tog-R, yo, k5, with CC k2tog-R, k1, with MC k1, with CC k1, yo, k1, with MC k1] six times, with CC k2.

Row 16 (WS): With CC k2, sm, [with MC p1, with CC p2, with MC p3, with CC p1, with MC p to last 7 sts before marker, with CC p2, with MC p2, with CC p2, with MC p1, sm] six times, with CC k2.

Row 15: With CC k2, sm, [with MC k2, with CC VDI, with MC k3, with CC k3tog-L, k1, with MC, k3, yo, VDD, yo, k7, yo, k2tog-R, yo, k5, yo, k1 yo, k3, yo, k1, yo, k5, yo, k2tog-L, yo, k7, yo, VDD, yo, k4, with CC k3tog-R, with MC k3, with CC VDI, with MC k2, sm] six times, with CC k2.

Row 16 (WS): With CC k2, sm, [with MC p2, with CC p3, with MC p3, with CC p1, with MC p to last 9 sts before marker, with CC p1, with MC p3, with CC p3, with MC p2, sm] six times, with CC k2.

Row 17: With CC k2, sm, [with MC, 2, with CC k1, VDI, k1, with MC k2, with CC k1, k3tog-L, with MC k2, VDD, k7, yo, k2tog-R, yo, k6, yo, k2tog-R, yo, k2tog-R, k1, k2tog-L, yo, k2tog-L, yo, k6, yo, k2tog-L, yo, k7, VDD, k2, with CC k3tog-R, k1, with MC k2, with CC k1, VDI, k1, with MC k2, sm] six times, with CC k2.

Row 18 (WS): With CC k2, sm, [with MC p2, with CC p5, with MC p2, with CC p2, with MC p to last 11 sts, with CC p2, with MC p2, with CC p5, with MC p2, sm] six times, with CC k2.

Row 19: With CC k2, sm, [with MC k3, with CC k1, VDI, k1, with MC k3, with CC k1, k3tog-L, k3, with MC k5, yo, k2tog-R, yo, k7, (yo, k2tog-R) twice, k1, (k2tog-L, yo) twice, k7, yo, k2tog-L, yo, k5, with CC k3, k3tog-R, k1, with MC k3, with CC k1, VDI, k1, with MC k3, sm] six times, with CC k2.

Row 20 (WS): With CC k2, sm, [p1, with MC p2, with CC p5, with MC p3, with CC p8, with MC p to last 19 sts, with CC p8, with MC p3, with CC p5, with MC p2, with CC p1, sm] six times, with CC k2.

Row 21: With CC k2, sm, [k1, with MC, k3, with CC k1, VDI, k1, with MC k4, with CC k1, k3tog-L, k7, with MC k to the last 22 sts, with CC k7, k3tog-R, k1, with MC k4, with CC k1, VDI, k1, with MC k3, with CC k1, sm] six times, with CC k2.

Row 22 (WS): With CC k2, sm, [p1, with MC p3, with CC p5, with MC p4, with CC p12, with MC p to last 25 sts, with CC p12, with MC p4, with CC p5, with MC p3, with CC p1, sm] six times, with CC k2—71 sts in each section, 430 sts total.

Next row (RS): K3, yo, [k 35, yo, k36] six times, yo—438 sts.

Next row (WS): Knit all sts.

LACE BOTTOM RUFFLE

Continue working with CC.

Row 1 (RS): Removing stitch markers as you work, k3, [wyws sl 1, k7, yo, k2tog-R, yo, k1, VDD, k1, yo, k2tog-L, yo, k7] 18 times, sl 1, k3.

Row 2 and all WS rows: K3, [p1, k11] 36 times, end p1, k3.

Row 3: [Wyws sl 1, k6, yo, k2tog-R, yo, k2, VDD, k2, yo, k2tog-L, yo, k6] 18 times, sl 1, k3.

Row 5: [Wyws sl 1, k5, yo, k2tog-R, yo, k3, VDD, k3, yo, k2tog-L, yo, k5] 18 times, sl 1, k3.

Row 7: [Wyws sl 1, k4, yo, k2tog-R, yo, k4, VDD, k4, yo, k2tog-L, yo, k4] 18 times, sl 1, k3.

Row 9: [Wyws sl 1, k3, yo, k2tog-R, yo, k5, VDD, k5, yo, k2tog-L, yo, k3] 18 times, sl 1, k3.

Row 11: [Wyws sl 1, k2, yo, k2tog-R, yo, k6, VDD, k6, yo, k2tog-L, yo, k2] 18 times, sl 1, k3.

Row 12 (WS): K3, p to last 3 sts, k3.

PICOT BIND-OFF

Next row (RS): Bind off all sts using the Picot Bind-Off as follows (see page 120 for photo-illustrated instructions).

1. K2tog-L.
2. Slip the st created back onto the LH needle and knit it.
3. Slip the st just created back onto the LH needle and knit it.
4. Slip the stitch created back onto the LH needle and work it, together with the next st, as a k2tog-L.

Rep steps 2–4 around work until all sts are bound off.

Weave in ends. Steam block.

Lace Bottom Ruffle
Multiple of 24 sts + 1

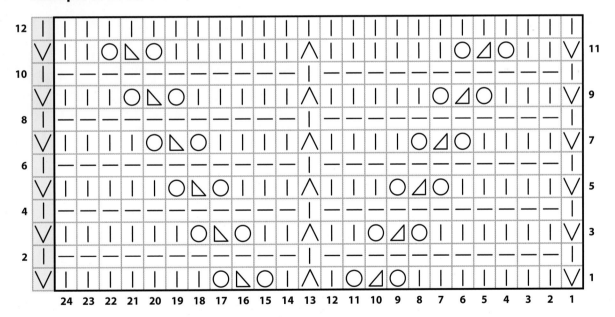

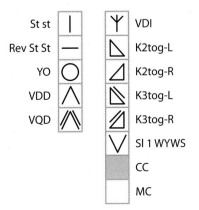

St st —	⅄ VDI
Rev St St	◹ K2tog-L
YO ○	◿ K2tog-R
VDD ∧	◩ K3tog-L
VQD ⋀⋀	⧄ K3tog-R
	∨ Sl 1 WYWS
	CC
	MC

Collar

Beg at Right Front edge (at garter rows dividing Section 2 from Section 3), with circ needle and using no yarn, PU 30 sts to start of initial CO sts. Carefully remove waste yarn from provisional CO and slip 22 CO sts onto needle. PU 30 sts down Left Front edge, ending at garter rows just past Section 2—82 sts total.

Slip sts back so you're ready to work a RS row (at Right Front).

SHORT-ROW SECTION 1

Note: There are several different ways to work a short row. You can choose to use the W&T method described here, or whichever technique you prefer.

Rows 1 and 2: K82.
Short Row 3 (RS): K79, W&T.
Short Row 4 (WS): K to 3 sts from end of row, W&T.
Short Row 5: K to 3 sts before last W&T, W&T.
Rep last row until 22 sts rem between W&Ts, end with a WS row.
Next row (RS): Knit to end of row, slipping each wrap up onto needle and working wrap along with stitch.
Next row (WS): Rep last row.

SHORT-ROW SECTION 2

Short Row 1 (RS): K80, W&T.
Short Row 2 (WS): K78, W&T.
Short Row 3: K to 2 sts before last W&T, W&T.
Rep last row until 42 sts rem between W&Ts, end with a WS row.
Next row (RS): Knit to end of row, slipping each wrap up onto needle and working wrap along with stitch.
Next row (WS): Rep last row.
BO all sts using a Picot Bind-Off as for hem of shawl.

Finishing

If desired, a small button can be sewn to the left front neck edge with a corresponding crocheted chain at the right neck edge.

Finished Measurements

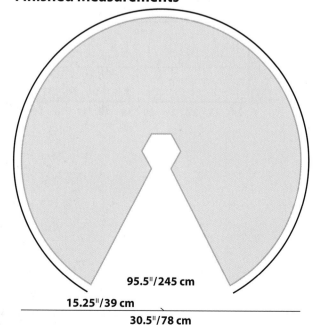

95.5"/245 cm

15.25"/39 cm

30.5"/78 cm

Striped Vertical
Crop Top

S ometimes an easy knit is exactly what the yarn requires! This very simple short sweater is unexpectedly flattering, and sets off a specialty yarn to perfection.

Finished Measurements

Bust: 28 (32, 36, 44, 48)"/71.5 (81.5, 92, 112, 122.5) cm
Body length: 7^1/$_2$ (9, 10^1/$_2$, 12, 13^1/$_2$)"/19 (23, 27, 30.5, 34.5) cm

Skill Level

Easy

Yarn

A Riot of Color Merino Worsted (100% wool; 216 yd./197 m per 3.5 oz/100 g skein)
• 2 (3, 3, 4, 5) skeins The Blues

Needles and Other Materials

• US 8 (5 mm) circular needle
• Yarn needle

Gauge

16 sts x 32 rows in St st/Garter patt = 4"/10 cm square
Adjust needle size if necessary to obtain gauge.

Stitch Guide

K2tog-L (knit 2 tog with a left slant)
Knit 2 stitches together so the working needle is pointing to the left as it enters the stitch (dec will slant to the left); common left-slanting decreases are ssk, k2tog-tbl, or skp.

K2tog-R (knit 2 tog with a right slant)
Knit 2 stitches together so the working needle is pointing to the right as it enters the stitch (dec will slant to the right); most common is k2tog.

Kfb (knit into front and back of one stitch)
Knit into the front and back of the same stitch—increase of 1 st.

PU&K (pick up & knit)
Insert needle into next stitch, stabbing all the way from the right side to the wrong side of the work. Wrap a loop around the needle and pull the loop through, creating a knit stitch.

Left Sleeve

With circular needles, CO 30 (32, 32, 34, 36) sts, join to work in the round, and place marker to note start of round.
Work in garter st for 4 rounds (knit 1 round, purl 1 round).
Begin Patt (worked in the round).
Rnds 1–5: Knit
Rnd 6: Purl
Rnds 7–8: Knit
Rep Rnds 1–8 while increasing every eighth round as foll:
Inc rnd: K2, kfb, k to 3 sts before marker, kfb, k2.
Cont inc on either side of marker every eighth round 23 (23, 24, 24, 24) times—76 (78, 80, 82, 84) sts.
Work even with no further increasing until sleeve meas 20 (21, 22, 23, 24)"/51 (53.5, 56, 58.5, 61) cm from cast on, ending with Rnd 5 of patt. (Make a note of how many rnds have been worked after the last increase.) Remove marker.

Body

Beg at point of marker CO 23 (23, 24, 24, 24) sts (Front of Body), turn work—99 (101, 104, 106, 108) sts.
Next row (WS): Knit the new sts plus the sleeve sts, then CO 23 (23, 24, 24, 24) sts (Back of Body)—122 (124, 128, 130, 132) sts.
Begin Patt (worked back and forth).
Rows 1 and all RS rows: Knit.
Rows 2 and 4 (WS): Purl.
Rows 6 and 8 (WS): Knit.
Rep Rows 1–8.
Cont working in patt as est for 64 (78, 88, 100, 114) rows from CO sts at end of sleeve. End with a WS row.

NECKLINE

Next row (RS): Cont in patt as est, work 61 (62, 64, 65, 66) sts. Join a second ball of yarn and work rem 61 (62, 64, 65, 66) sts.
Cont working the two equal halves of the work separately, creating a slit along the center of the work, until the neck opening meas 26 (30, 34, 40, 46)"/66.5 (76.5, 86.5, 102, 117.5) cm. End with a WS row.

Next row (RS): Cont in patt as est, work across all sts with a single ball of yarn, break yarn from second ball and set aside.

Work in patt as est for approx 64 (78, 88, 100, 114) rows from end of neck opening. End with Row 6 of patt.

Next row (WS): BO 23 (23, 24, 24, 24) sts, knit to end of row—99 (101, 104, 106, 108) sts rem.

Next row (RS): BO 23 (23, 24, 24, 24) sts, knit to end of row—76 (78, 80, 82, 84) sts rem.

Right Sleeve

Return to circ needle and place marker to note start of round (underarm point).

Work in patt in the round as est, working the same number of non-shaped rows as you ended with at the end of the Left Sleeve (the number of rows noted above).

Working in patt as est, dec 1 st at either side of the marker every 8th round as foll:

Dec rnd: K2, k2tog-L, knit to 4 sts before marker, k2tog-R, k2.

Cont dec on either side of marker every 8th round 23 (23, 24, 24, 24) times—30 (32, 32, 34, 36) sts rem. Work in garter for 4 rounds. Bind off all sts loosely.

Neck Facing

Return to neck opening and starting at one corner, with circ needle PU&K 52 (60, 68, 80, 92) sts around entire neckline.

Knit 6 rounds.

Purl 1 round.

Knit 6 rounds.

Bind off all sts loosely.

Steam Neck Facing, turn under and sew the bound-off edge to the underside of the neck opening.

Hem

Steam block piece. Sew side seams together.

Beg at one seam, PU&K 360 (360, 384, 384, 384) sts around entire hem.

Knit 6 rounds, then work 4 rounds in garter stitch. BO all sts loosely.

Finishing

Weave in ends. Steam block piece again.

Finished Measurements

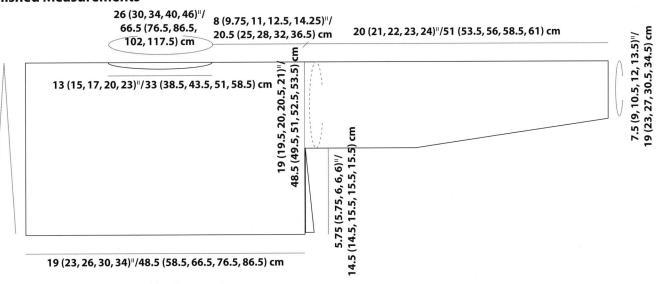

Sweet Lace Bolero

charming little lace top, this would be as at home over a pair of jeans and camisole as it would be dressing up a sleeveless cocktail dress. The repeating lace pattern, echoed in the sleeves, decreases in pattern creating an elegantly diminishing yoke.

Sizes

To fit chest 34 (38, 42, 46, 50, 54)"/87 (97, 107, 117, 128, 138) cm

Finished Measurements

Bust: $38^{1}/_{4}$ ($41^{3}/_{4}$, $45^{1}/_{4}$, $48^{3}/_{4}$, $52^{1}/_{4}$, $55^{3}/_{4}$)"/98 (107, 115, 124, 133, 142) cm

Skill Level

Advanced

Yarn

Bijou Basin Ranch Lhasa Wilderness, fine weight #2 yarn (75% yak, 25% bamboo; 180 yd./164 m per 2 oz./57 g skein)
• 3 (4, 5, 5, 6, 6) skeins Blueberry

Needles and Other Materials

• US 7 (4.5 mm) needles
• 2 stitch markers
• Yarn needle
• Waste yarn

Gauge

16 sts x 28 rows in St st = 4"/10 cm square
Adjust needle size if necessary to obtain gauge.

Stitch Guide

K2tog-L (knit 2 tog with a left slant)
Knit 2 stitches together so the working needle is pointing to the left as it enters the stitch (dec will slant to the left); common left-slanting decreases are ssk, k2tog-tbl, or skp.

K2tog-R (knit 2 tog with a right slant)
Knit 2 stitches together so the working needle is pointing to the right as it enters the stitch (dec will slant to the right); most common is k2tog.

VDD (vertical double decrease)
Sl 2 sts as if to work k2tog-R, k1, pass slipped sts over—decrease of 2 sts.

Body

CO 150 (162, 178, 190, 206, 218) sts.
Row 1 (RS): [K2, p2] rep to end, end k2.
Row 2 (WS): K2, [k2, p2] rep to last 2 sts, end k2.
Rep last 2 rows twice more, 6 rib rows total. Inc 3 (5, 3, 5, 3, 5) sts evenly across last rib row—153 (167, 181, 195, 209, 223) sts.

LACE PATTERN

Work Rows 1–2 of Lace Chart (between brackets in pattern) as foll:
Row 1 (RS): K5, pm, [k1, sl 1, k1, k2tog-R twice, [yo, k1] 3 times, yo, k2tog-L twice] rep 10 (11, 12, 13, 14, 15) times to last 8 sts, k1, sl 1, k1, pm, k5.
Row 2 and all WS rows: K5, sm, [purl to next marker], sm, k5.
Rep last 2 rows until piece meas 13 (14, 17, 18, 19, 22)"/33 (36, 43, 46, 48, 56) cm from cast-on edge, set aside.

Sweet Lace Bolero Chart

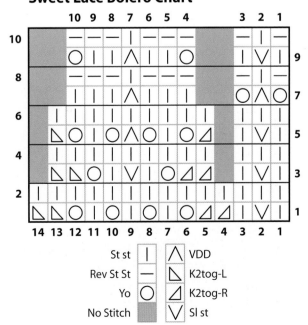

Sleeve (Make 2)

CO 56 (68, 68, 84, 84, 84) sts.

Row 1 (RS): [K2, p2] rep around all sts.

Cont in rib for a total of 6 rounds. Inc 0 (2, 2, 0, 0, 0) sts
evenly across last rib row—56 (70, 70, 84, 84, 84) sts total.

LACE PATTERN

Rnd 1: [K1, sl 1, k1, k2tog-R twice, yo, k1, yo, k1, yo, k1, yo,
k2tog-L twice] rep around all sts 4 (5, 5, 6, 6, 6) times.

Rnd 2 and all even rnds: Knit all sts.

Rep last 2 rnds until piece meas 2 (2, 2^1/$_2$, 2^1/$_2$, 3, 3^1/$_2$)"/5 (5,
6, 6, 8, 9) cm from cast-on edge. Slip the first 14 (14, 14, 28,
28, 28) sts onto a piece of waste yarn (underarm sts). Set
aside sleeve.

JOINING SLEEVES TO BODY

Return to body. Cont in patt as est, work across first 33 (33,
47, 33, 33, 47) Front sts, slip next 14 (14, 14, 28, 28, 28) sts
onto a piece of waste yarn. Work 42 (56, 56, 56, 56, 56)
from one sleeve (the waste yarn sts should align at the
underarm), cont in patt as est, return to body sts.

Work across next 59 (73, 59, 73, 87, 73) Back Sts in patt as
est. Work 42 (56, 56, 56, 56, 56) from one sleeve (the waste
yarn sts should align at the underarm), cont in patt as est,
return to body sts. Slip next 14 (14, 14, 28, 28, 28) sts onto
waste yarn, work rem 33 (33, 47, 33, 33, 47) Front sts—209
(251, 265, 251, 265, 279) Yoke Sts total.

Yoke

Cont working first two rows of Lace Chart in patt as est
until piece meas 4^1/$_4$ (4^3/$_4$, 5^1/$_4$, 5^3/$_4$, 6^1/$_4$, 6^3/$_4$)"/11 (12, 13,
15, 16, 17) cm from Sleeve join.

FIRST YOKE DECREASE

Work Rows 3–4 of Lace Chart (between brackets) across all sts as foll:

Row 3 (RS): K5, sm, [k1, sl 1, k1, k2tog-R twice, yo, k1, sl 1, k1, yo, k2tog-L twice] rep 14 (17, 18, 17, 18, 19) times to last 8 sts, k1, sl 1, k1, sm, k5—181 (217, 229, 217, 229, 241).

Rows 4 and 6 (WS): K5, sm, [purl to next marker], sm, k5.

Row 5 (RS): K5, sm, [k1, sl 1, k1, k2tog-R, yo, k1, yo, VDD, yo, k1, yo, k2tog-L] rep 14 (17, 18, 17, 18, 19) times to last 8 sts, k1, sl 1, k1, sm, k5.

Rep Rows 5–6 until piece meas $2^{1}/_{8}$ ($2^{3}/_{8}$, $2^{5}/_{8}$, $2^{7}/_{8}$, $3^{1}/_{8}$, $3^{3}/_{8}$)"/5 (6, 7, 7, 8, 9) cm from First Yoke Dec.

SECOND YOKE DECREASE

Cont in chart as est.

Row 7 (RS): K5, sm, [yo, VDD, yo, k3, VDD, k3] rep 14 (17, 18, 17, 18, 19) times to last 8 sts, yo, VDD, yo, sm, k5—153 (183, 193, 183, 193, 203) rem.

Rows 8 and 10: K5, sm, k1, p1, k1, [k3, p1, k4, p1, k1] rep 14 (17, 18, 17, 18, 19) times, sm, k5.

Row 9 (RS): K5, sm, [k1, sl 1, k1, yo, k2, VDD, k2, yo] rep 14 (17, 18, 17, 18, 19) times to last 8 sts, k1, sl 1, k1, sm, k5.

Rep Rows 9–10 until piece meas $2^{1}/_{4}$ ($2^{1}/_{2}$, $2^{1}/_{2}$, 3, 3, 3)"/6 (6, 6, 8, 8, 8) cm from Second Yoke Dec.

Work 4 rows of garter st (knit each row). Bind off all sts.

Finishing

Slip underarm sts from sleeve and underarm sts from body onto two separate needles.

Work underarm sts tog in a 3-needle bind-off as follows (see page 119 for photo-illustrated instructions), using the tails at the start and end of BO to tidy up any open spaces at each armhole.

1. Place the two pieces to be joined on knitting needles so the right sides of each piece are facing each other with the needles parallel.
2. Insert a third needle one size larger through the leading edge of the first stitch on each needle (knitwise).
3. Knit these stitches together as one, leaving 1 st on RH needle.
4. Repeat steps 2–3, and slip the older stitch on RH needle over newer stitch.

Repeat step 4 until all sts are bound off. Cut yarn, pull through last stitch.

Finished Measurements

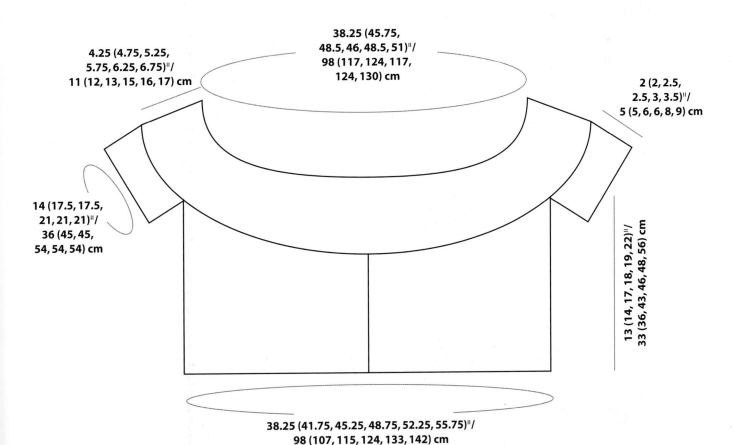

4.25 (4.75, 5.25, 5.75, 6.25, 6.75)"/ 11 (12, 13, 15, 16, 17) cm

38.25 (45.75, 48.5, 46, 48.5, 51)"/ 98 (117, 124, 117, 124, 130) cm

2 (2, 2.5, 2.5, 3, 3.5)"/ 5 (5, 6, 6, 8, 9) cm

14 (17.5, 17.5, 21, 21, 21)"/ 36 (45, 45, 54, 54, 54) cm

13 (14, 17, 18, 19, 22)"/ 33 (36, 43, 46, 48, 56) cm

38.25 (41.75, 45.25, 48.75, 52.25, 55.75)"/ 98 (107, 115, 124, 133, 142) cm

Tasseled Hooded Scarf

he simple shape of this piece is deceptive. All of the drama comes from the cables, which are a delightful counterpoint to the whimsical tassels at the tip of the hood and bottom edge of the scarf.

Finished Measurements

Scarf width: 7$\frac{1}{2}$"/19 cm
Scarf length: 51$\frac{1}{2}$"/131.5 cm
Hood length: 12"/30.5 cm

Skill Level

Advanced

Yarn

ModeKnit Yarn ModeWerk Worsted, medium weight #4 yarn (100% superwash merino wool, 176 yd./162 m per 3.5 oz./100 g skein)
• 2 skeins Pearl

Needles and Other Materials

• US 8 (5 mm) needles

Gauge

26 sts x 28 rows in Cable patt with US 8 needles = 4"/10 cm
Adjust needle size if necessary to obtain gauge.

Stitch Guide

C2/1pL (cable 2k and 1p st with left twist)
Sl 2 sts and hold to front, p1, k slipped sts.

C2/1pR (cable 2k and 1p st with right twist)
Sl 1 purl st and hold to back, k2, p slipped st.

C2R (cable 2 sts with right twist)
Move yarn to RS, sl 1 st and hold to back, k1, k slipped st.

C4R (cable 4 with a right twist)
Move yarn to RS, sl 2 sts and hold to back, k2, k slipped sts.

C6L (cable 6 with a left twist)
Sl 3 sts and hold to front, k3, k slipped sts.

continued

Dkss Edge (double knit slipped st edge, worked over 3 sts)

This edging is created by slipping and knitting stitches, keeping in mind that whenever stitches are slipped at either 3-st edge, the yarn is held *toward* the knitter, regardless of whether the right or wrong side is facing the knitter. On the RS rows, at either end, the 3 edge sts are worked knit, slip, knit. On the WS rows, at either end, the 3 edge sts are worked slip, knit, slip.

RS Row: {K1, wyrs sl 1, k1}, work to last 3 sts, {k1, wyrs sl 1, k1}.

WS Row: {Wyws sl 1, k1, wyws sl 1}, work to last 3 sts, {wyws sl 1, k1, wyws sl 1}.

Kfb (knit into front and back of one stitch)

Knit into the front and back of the same stitch—increase of 1 st.

PU (pick up)

Using the knitting needle only, with no source of yarn, pick up a loop from the existing fabric to create a stitch on the needle.

Wyrs Sl 1 (with yarn right side, slip 1)

Move yarn to RS of work. Insert RH needle purlwise into st and slip onto RH needle.

Wyws Sl 1 (with yarn wrong side, slip 1)

Move yarn to WS of work. Insert RH needle purlwise into st and slip onto RH needle.

Scarf

With a piece of waste yarn, provisionally cast on 48 sts (see page 118 for how to work a provisional cast-on).

72-ROW CABLE PATTERN

Follow Cable Chart or written instructions as foll:

Row 1: {K1, wyrs sl 1, k1}, k2, sl 1, [p3, k6, p3] rep to last 6 sts, sl 1, k2 {k1, wyrs sl 1, k1}.

Row 2 and all WS rows: {Wyws sl 1, k1, wyws sl 1}, k2, p1, work in rib as est to last 6 sts, p1, k2, {wyws sl 1, k1, wyws sl 1}.

Row 3: {Dkss RS edge}, k2, sl 1, [p3, C6L, p3] rep to last 6 sts, sl 1, k2, {dkss RS edge}.

Row 5: Rep Row 1.

Work Rows 1–6 three times.

Row 7: {Dkss RS edge}, k2, sl 1, [p2, C2/1pR, k2, C2/1pL, p2] rep to last 6 sts, sl 1, k2, {dkss RS edge}.

Row 9: {Dkss RS edge}, k2, sl 1, [p1, C2/1pR, p1, k2, p1, C2/1pL, p1] rep to last 6 sts, sl 1, k2, {dkss RS edge}.

Row 11: {Dkss RS edge}, k2, sl 1, [C2/1pR, p2, k2, p2, C2/1pL] rep to last 6 sts, sl 1, k2, {dkss RS edge}.

Row 13: {Dkss RS edge}, k2, sl 1, k2, p3, C2R, p3, [C4R, p3, C2R, p3] rep to last 20 sts, C4R, p3, C2R, p3, k2, sl 1, k2, {dkss RS edge}.

Row 15: {Dkss RS edge}, k2, sl 1, [k2, p3, k2, p3, k2] rep to last 6 sts, sl 1, k2, {dkss RS edge}.

Work Rows 13–16 four times.

Row 17: {Dkss RS edge}, k2, sl 1, k2, p3, C2R, p3, [C4R, p3, C2R, p3] rep to last 20 sts, C4R, p3, C2R, p3, k2, sl 1, k2, {dkss RS edge}.

Row 19: {Dkss RS edge}, k2, sl 1, [C2/1pL, p2, k2, p2, C2/1pR] rep to last 6 sts, sl 1, k2, {dkss RS edge}.

Row 21: {Dkss RS edge}, k2, sl 1, [p1, C2/1pL, p1, k2, p1, C2/1pR, p1] rep to last 6 sts, sl 1, k2, {dkss RS edge}.

Row 23: {Dkss RS edge}, k2, sl 1, [p2, C2/1pL, k2, C2/1pR, p2] rep to last 6 sts, sl 1, k2, {dkss RS edge}.

Row 25: Rep Row 1.

Row 27: Rep Row 3.

Row 29: Rep Row 1.

Work Rows 25–30 three times.

Repeat all rows of the Tassled Scarf Chart five times (repeating the sections as directed, the total rows per repeat will be 72, 360 rows total), ending with Row 30 of the Cable Chart.

Bind off all sts using an I-cord bind-off, as follows. Slip provisionally CO sts onto needle and bind these off with I-cord bind-off as well.

I-Cord Bind-Off

To start, cast on 3 sts at start of row.
1. K2, k2tog-L.
2. Slip 3 sts from RH needle back onto LH needle.
3. Pull yarn taut across back of work.
4. Repeat steps 1–3 across work until 3 sts rem.
5. End k3tog-L, tie off last stitch.

Cable Chart

C6L
C4R
C2/1pL
C2/1pR
C2R

St st | |
Rev St St | —
Sl st (wyws) | ∨
Sl st (wyrs) | ⋏

3 x 6 rows
18 rows total

4 x 4 rows
16 rows total

3 x 6 rows
18 rows total

Hood

Fold the scarf in half and mark the center point. It should be in the center of a Row 13-16 repeat section. Place a marker along one edge to note the lengthwise center of the scarf.

Working from this center point, PU 27 sts along the scarf edge on either side of the marker, 54 sts total.

Next row (RS): [Kfb] 18 times, k6, [kfb] 6 times, k6, [kfb] 18 times—96 sts.

Next row (WS): Purl all sts.

Work in charted patt as written above across all sts, working dkss edge at either end, and repeating sts 19–30 of chart five times across work between initial and final 18 sts. Work even with no increasing or decreasing until hood meas 12"/30 cm from picked up sts, or desired length. End with a WS row.

Next row (RS): Arrange sts so half are on one needle and half on a separate needle. Using a third needle, and with the right sides of the hood facing toward each other (WS facing out) join all the stitches in a 3-needle bind-off, as follows (see page 119 for photo-illustrated instructions).

1. Place the two pieces to be joined on knitting needles so the right sides of each piece are facing each other with the needles parallel.

2. Insert a third needle one size larger through the leading edge of the first stitch on each needle (knitwise).

3. Knit these stitches together as one, leaving 1 st on RH needle.

4. Repeat steps 2–3, slip the older stitch on RH needle over newer stitch.

Repeat step 4 until all sts are bound off. Cut yarn, pull through last stitch.

Tassels and Finishing
(Make 5)

Find a book, piece of wood or other item which is narrow and approx 8"/20 cm wide. Wrap yarn around this item 48 times. Carefully remove the yarn from the book and tie all strands together 1"/2.5 cm down from one end. Cut the loops at the opposite end, trim the ends to even up the tassel.

Sew two tassels to each end of the scarf corresponding to the outermost cables. Sew the final tassel to the tip of the hood.

Weave in ends. Steam block entire piece.

Finished Measurements

13.5"/34.5 cm

12"/30.5 cm

7.5"/19 cm

51.5"/131.5 cm

How to Use This Book

Styles of Knitting

It's a lesser known knitting fact that there are several perfectly valid ways to create knit and purl stitches. The majority of knitters reading this would be what Priscilla Gibson Roberts, in her exceptional book *Knitting In The Old Way*, describes as Western knitters. Other common styles of knitting include Eastern and Combination (also known as Eastern Uncrossed). Most knitting books are written from the point of view of a Western knitter. This book will be an exception. These style designations have nothing to do with how a knitter holds their yarn; yarn can be held successfully in either the left or right hand for any of these knitting styles. The difference lies in the actual stitch construction.

The smallest group of knitters are those who form their stitches in the Eastern style. In Eastern knitting, each stitch is twisted, giving the fabric a more woven appearance, with less elasticity and a firmer drape than Western knitting.

A growing group are the Combination, or Eastern Uncrossed, knitters. This style marries the Eastern purl with the Western knit, creating a fabric that resembles Western knitting in appearance and drape, but when working back and forth the stitches are formed in a different manner.

At the start of the 20th Century, modern printing enabled the beginning of a mass knitting pattern publishing industry (fueled by gravure presses and originating in Western nations). The pattern industry designated Western knitting as the "standard" method of creating a knit stitch. It's a small step from "the standard way" to "the right way," and unfortunately, for most of the 20th Century other methods of knitting were seen as lesser, or not quite correct.

In order to make my patterns accessible to all knitters, I steer away from stitch instructions that explain *how* to make a stitch, favoring instructions that simply name the stitch or the desired result of the stitch. Thus, a knitter of any style—including Western knitters—can easily follow the instructions to the intended result. If any of the terms or stitches used in this book are unfamiliar to you, refer to the Stitch Guide for the project, Terms and Abbreviations (page 124), or this reference section to find the help you need.

How to Read a Chart

I love charts. I believe charts are one of the great milestones in modern knitting, allowing every type of knitter to work up a motif no matter what language they speak.

A chart may seem confusing at first glance, but with a little study it will reveal the logic of a stitch or colorwork motif. The chart is a symbolic illustration of the Right Side (RS) of the work—hence why a vertical line in a chart labeled St st (stockinette stitch) means knit on the right side but purl on the wrong side (so that the knit side of the stitch, the V shape, will be on the right side). Take a few minutes, familiarize yourself with the symbols in a specific chart, and begin working as intuitively as you can.

Every charted motif should include a graphic stitch key. A stitch key shows an example of the stitch, lists any abbreviations used in the written instructions for the stitch, and also sometimes gives a written description of how to work the stitch or technique. I favor having a symbol in each square of a chart with grayed areas for stitches which are "missing" due to decreases, or to note stitches which haven't yet been created in the current row.

It's helpful to use a sticky note to mark rows, I like to keep the sticky part of the note to the bottom, aligned to the upper edge of the current row. This allows me to see the rows that have been worked (so I can compare the fabric on my needle to the finished chart rows) and also make notations on any unusual symbols.

When reading a chart, work from the bottom up, and read the rows in the same direction as you are working your fabric. When knitting back and forth, Row 1 and all odd rows would be worked as a RS row (read the chart from right to left), Row 2 and all even rows would be worked as a WS row (read the chart from left to right). When working in the round, all rows of the chart would be read from right to left.

Techniques

There are a few techniques that I use that you may not be familiar with, and several of them are covered in this section. However, if there are other techniques you don't know or if a video tutorial would be helpful, do a quick Internet search and you will find what you are looking for.

DECREASES

There are three basic decreases that are worked in knitting.

- **Decreases that slant to the right.** Often known simply as k2tog, I like to call this decrease K2tog-R. In Western knitting, the stitches are already seated to work a k2tog-R. As the needle enters the stitches to be decreased, the tip of the working needle* will point to the right in this decrease. In Combination knitting, the stitches must be reoriented so they're seated to slant easily to the right.
- **Decreases that slant to the left.** Ssk (slip, slip knit), k2tog-tbl (knit 2 tog through the back loop), and skp (slip, knit, pass slipped st over the knit stitch) are three different ways to work what I call k2tog-L. As a general rule of thumb, if you're a Western knitter, when you see the term k2tog-L, work it as an ssk.
- **Decreases that stand straight up and don't slant.** Known as VDD (vertical double decrease) or CDD (centered double decrease), a vertical decrease will always be comprised of an odd number of stitches as one stitch has to act as the center point of the decrease.

---

* The working needle is the needle which is not holding the stitches, the needle that actually does the work. For most knitters the working needle will be the right-hand needle. For left-handed knitters, the working needle is often the left-hand needle.

PROVISIONAL CAST-ON

This is a term used to describe a cast-on which can be easily removed later, leaving a row of live stitches to be slipped onto a needle and worked. One favorite method is to crochet a chain in waste yarn with at least ten more stitches than are required. Tie off the end of the chain, placing a knot in the tail. Slip your knitting needle into the bump at the back of each chain, creating a "stitch" on the needle. When desired, the chain can be loosened and pulled off at the knotted end, leaving live stitches to work into.

1. Crochet a chain in waste yarn with at least ten more stitches than are required and tie off, placing a knot in the tail.

2. Slip your knitting needle into the bump at the back of each chain to create a "stitch."

I-CORD BIND-OFF

To start, cast on 3 stitches at start of row/round.
1. K2, k2tog-L.
2. Slip 3 sts from RH needle back onto LH needle.
3. Pull yarn taut across back of work.
4. Repeat steps 1–3 across work until 3 sts rem.
5. End k3tog-L, tie off last stitch.

3-NEEDLE BIND-OFF

1. Place the two pieces to be joined on knitting needles so the right sides of each piece are facing each other with the needles parallel. Insert a third needle one size larger through the leading edge of the first stitch on each needle (knitwise).

2. Knit these stitches together as one, leaving 1 st on RH needle.

3. Again, insert the spare needle through the leading edge of the first stitch on each needle and knit them together.

4. Slip the older stitch on RH needle over newer stitch and off the needle.
   Repeat steps 3–4 until all sts are bound off. Cut yarn, pull through last stitch.

continued

5. The bind-off from the wrong and right sides.

K2TOG BIND-OFF

1. K2tog-L.
2. Slip the stitch created back onto the LH needle.
Rep steps 1–2 until all sts are bound off. Tie off last st.

PICOT BIND-OFF

1. K2tog-L.

2. Slip the st created back onto the left needle and knit it.

3. Repeat step 2 as many times as you wish.

4. Slip the stitch created back onto the left needle and work it, together with the next st, as a k2tog-L. Repeat steps 2–4 around work until all sts are bound off. In this photo, 2 stitches are bound off between picots.

CABLES

A cable is a stitch motif worked to emulate the appearance of a cabled rope. To do this, a group of stitches is divided into two smaller groups with either the first group crossing in front of the second group (Cable Front or Cable Left) or the first group traveling behind the second group (Cable Back or Cable Right). I like to use the directional terms Cable Left and Cable Right as these are more universal and make sense to every type of knitter.

Here is a charted 4-st cable. Notice that the first group of stitches crosses in front of the second group of stitches. This can be written as C4L (C4Left) or C4F (C4Front).

In the second 4-st cable, the first group of stitches travels behind the second group of stitches. This can be written as C4R (C4Right) or C4B (C4Back).

Cabling with a Cable Needle

Often the first group of stitches is slipped onto a smaller needle, known as a cable needle, which is held to the front or to the back while the second group of stitches is worked to create the cable. I generally don't use a cable needle because I feel it can make a cable too loose and uneven, but I know that many folks prefer to work cables in this manner.

Cabling without a Cable Needle

Cable Front or Left Cable

1. Slip the first group to be cabled to the RH needle. Knit the second group of stitches.

2. Slide the LH needle across the front and into the stitches that were originally skipped.

3. Form an X with the needles.

continued

4. Squeeze the knit fabric just below the X.

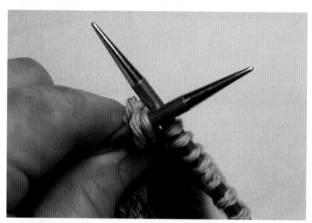

5. Carefully pull the RH needle out of *all* stitches involved in the cable. The stitches that had been knitted will be free, but not loose (not if you're holding tight!).

6. Pick up these free stitches with the RH needle. Knit the originally slipped stitches which now wait on the LH needle.

7. The completed cable.

Cable Back or Right Cable

1. Bring the yarn to the front of the work.
2. Slip the first group to be cabled to the RH needle.
3. Knit the second group of stitches, bring the yarn to the front of the work.
4. Slide the LH needle across the back and into the stitches that were originally skipped.
5. Form an X with the needles.
6. Squeeze the knit fabric just below the X.
7. Carefully pull the RH needle out of all stitches involved in the cable.
8. Pick up these free stitches with the RH needle (they'll be in the front).
9. Knit the originally slipped stitches which now wait on the LH needle.

Multiple Strand Cables

When working a cable with more than two groups of stitches crossing each other, the trick is to use multiple cable needles, as in the C11 Center St cable from the Cross Body Wrap.

1. Sl 5 sts to cable needle and hold to back.
2. Sl 1 st to second cable needle and hold to front.
3. K5.
4. K1 from front cable needle.
5. K5 from back cable needle.

PICKING UP STITCHES

1. Insert needle into loop in fabric.

2. Loops from fabric aligned on needle.

SHORT ROWS (WRAP & TURN)

1. Work to turning point, bring yarn to front.

2. Slip next st to RH needle.

3. Move yarn to back, slip st back onto LH needle.

4. Short rows worked at 8-stitch intervals.

Terms and Abbreviations

Abbreviation	Term	Description
BO	Bind off	
C2/1pL	Cable 2k and 1p st with left twist	Sl 2 sts and hold to front, p1, k slipped sts
C2/1pR	Cable 2k and 1p st with right twist	Sl 1 purl st and hold to back, p2, p slipped st
C2R	Cable 2 sts with right twist	Move yarn to RS, sl 1 st and hold to back, k1, k slipped st
C3pL	Cable 3 sts with left twist, purling back st	Sl 2 sts and hold to front of work, p1, k slipped st
C3pR	Cable 3 sts with right twist, purling back st	Sl 1 st and hold to back of work, k2, purl slipped st
C4L	Cable 4 left	Sl 2 sts and hold to front, k2, k slipped sts
C4R	Cable 4 right	Move yarn to RS, sl 2 sts and hold to back, k2, k slipped sts
C6L	Cable 6 left	Sl 3 sts and hold to front, k3, k slipped sts
Circ	Circular needle	
CO	Cast on	
Cont	Continue	
Dkss RS/WS Edge	Double knit slipped st edge	Usually a three-stitch technique; on the RS rows the three edge stitches are worked knit, slip, knit. On the WS rows the three edge stitches are worked slip, knit, slip. The main thing to remember when working this edge is that whenever a stitch is slipped, the yarn will be held *toward* the knitter. You will see this edge designated in patterns as {dkss RS/WS edge}.
Est	Established	
Foll	Follows/following	
Hdc	Half double crochet	Yarn over hook. Insert hook in the next st to be worked. Yarn over hook. Pull yarn through st. Yarn over hook. Pull yarn through all 3 loops on hook (one hdc made).
K	Knit	Insert needle into st from front to back, yo, pull loop through st and kick old stitch off of needle
K2tog-L	Knit 2 tog with left slant	Knit 2 sts together so the working needle is pointing to the left as it enters the sts (dec sts will slant to the left); ssk
K2tog-R	Knit 2 tog with right slant	Knit 2 sts together so the working needle is pointing to the right as it enters the st (dec sts will slant to the right); k2tog
K3tog-L	Knit 3 tog with left slant	Knit 3 sts together so they slant to the left when viewed from RS of work; sssk
K3tog-R	Knit 3 tog with right slant	Knit 3 sts together so they slant to the right when viewed from RS of work; k3tog
Kfb	Knit front and back	Knit into the front and back of one st, then kick that st off the needle—inc of 1 st
LH	Left hand	
Meas	Measures	
P	Purl	Insert needle into st from back to front, yo, pull loop through st and kick old stitch off of needle
P2tog	Purl 2 together	Working on WS of piece, insert needle into 2 sts from back to front, yo, pull loop through both sts and kick old sts off of needle. Dec sts will slant to the right when viewed from RS of work.

Terms and Abbreviations continued

Abbreviation	Term	Description
P2tog-tbl	Purl 2 tog through the back loop	Working on the WS of piece, purl 2 sts together so the working needle is pointing to the right as it enters the sts (needle enters the second st on LH needle, then the first st on LH needle). Dec sts will slant to the left when viewed from RS.
Patt	Pattern	
Pfb	Purl front and back	Purl into the front and back of one st, then kick that st off the needle—inc of 1 st
Pm	Place marker	
PU	Pick up	Using the knitting needle only, with no source of yarn, pick up a loop from the existing fabric to create a st on the needle
PU&K	Pick up and knit	Using a separate source of yarn, insert the knitting needle from the front to the back of the work, yo, pull loop through creating a st on the needle
PU&P	Pick up and purl	Using a separate source of yarn, insert the knitting needle from the back to the front of the work, yo, pull loop through creating a st on the needle
Rev St st	Reverse stockinette stitch	Purl on the RS, knit on the WS
RH	Right hand	
Rib	Ribbing	A repeating pattern of knit and purl sts juxtaposed against each other to create a decorative pattern
RS	Right side	
Sc	Single crochet	Insert hook in st. Yarn over hook. Pull yarn through st. Yarn over hook. Pull yarn through 2 loops on hook (one sc made).
Sl	Slip	Move yarn to WS of work. Insert RH needle purlwise into st and slip off of LH needle.
Sm	Slip marker	
Ssk	Slip, slip, knit	Slip 1 st as if to knit, sl another st as if to knit, move both sts back onto LH needle and knit both tog through the back loop
St st	Stockinette stitch	Knit on the RS, purl on the WS
VDD	Vertical double decrease	Slip 2 sts as if to work a k2tog-R, knit the next st, pass the slipped sts over the knit st—dec of 2 sts
VDI	Vertical double increase	Knit into front of st, yo, knit into back of same st—inc of 2 sts
VQD	Vertical quad decrease	Sl 3 sts as if to work k3tog-R, k2tog-L, pass slipped sts over knit st—dec of 4 sts
W&T	Wrap and turn	Work the desired number of sts for the short row. Move yarn to RS. Slip next st to the RH needle. Move yarn to WS. Return st to LH needle. Turn and begin working back in the opposite direction.
WS	Wrong side	
Wyrs	With yarn right side	Hold the yarn to the RS of the work
Wyws	With yarn wrong side	Hold the yarn to the WS of the work
Yo	Yarn over	Wrap yarn around the needle in the same direction as you wrapped the previous st

Visual Index

Basketweave Bolero   1

Cabled Poncho Set   5

Chevron Cowled Poncho   13

Colorwork Ruana   17

Cross Body Wrap & Scarf   22

Entrelac Poncho   28

Fitted Lace Off-Shoulder Top   39

Funnel Neck Twisted Float Armery   44

Log Cabin Cardigan   49

Lace Cuff Shrug   55

Lace Knit Shrug   59

Mitered Ruana   63

Morse Cowl   68

Plaid Vest   71

Short Kimono Cardigan   76

Stained Glass Armery   79

Stained Glass Circular Jacket   83

Strasbourg Cape   95

Striped Vertical Crop Top   105

Sweet Lace Bolero   108

Tasseled Hooded Scarf   112

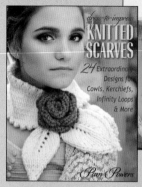